C000019269

RELISH YORKSHIRE SECOND HELPING

Original recipes from the region's finest chefs

First Published 2010
By Relish Publications
Shield Green Farm, Tritlington,
Northumberland NE61 3DX

ISBN 978-0-9564205-3-4

Publisher: Duncan L Peters
General Manager: Teresa Baughan
Marketing and Design Manager: Ria Parkin
Photography: Adrian Gatie
Printed By: Balto Print Ltd, Stratford,
London E15 2TF

RELISH
PUBLICATIONS.CO.UK

004 CONTENTS

PAGE	STARTERS	MAINS
008-017	Poached Guinea Fowl and Basil Terrine, Sloe Gin Jelly, Pickled Sultanas, Confit Orange	Venison Loin and Shoulder, Potato Wall, Mulled Winter Fruits, Chocolate Candy
018-027	Roast Breast of Wood Pigeon with Crispy Leg Meat, Beetroot and Dried Fruit Purée	Roasted Thorpe Underwood Venison with a Baby Shepherd's Pie, Chocolate Jelly, Fondant Vegetables, Sauce Cassis
028-037	Dressed Crab with Braised Chicken Hearts, Cocks Crest and Basil and Lemon Sorbet	Pork 5 Ways
038-047	Pan Seared Scallops with Spiced Aubergines, Chestnut Purée and Salted Hazelnuts	Pan Fried Fillet of East Coast Cod, with a Goat's Cheese Crust, Lemon Thyme Mash, Watercress Beignet and Roast Tomato Oil
048-057	Seared Scallop, Celeriac, Apple, Smoked Eel, Truffle	Lamb Textures
058-067	Smoking Venison Carpaccio	Plate of Pig
068-077	King Prawns	Guancia Di Buebrasata
078-087	Grilled Gambas with Chorizo Butter, Lemon and Aioli	Seabass with Charlotte Potatoes, Mussels and Chorizo
088-097	Wild Mushroom Basket	Estbek's Seafood Pie
098-107	East Coast Crab, Tomato and Avocado, Salsa and Brown Crab Dressing	Harewood Estate Venison Cooked Two Ways
108-117	Rabbit and Plum Tart, Yorkshire Blue and Mustard Sauce, Hot Apple Jelly	Roasted Breast of Pheasant, Rolled Thigh Stuffed with Black Pudding, Lollipop Leg, Soured White Cabbage, Ale Jus
118-127	Pan Seared King Scallops, Caramelised Cauliflower Purée, Black Pudding	Pan Roasted Duck Breast, Peppered Swede, Chestnut Crusted Parsnips, Mulled Wine Jus
128-137	Roast Fillet of Whitby Cod with Yorkshire Liquorice Sauce, Caramelised Cob Nuts and Parsnip Crisps	Roast Ridgeway Partridge wrapped in Proscuitto Sautéed Porcini and Black Pudding, Crab Apple and Thyme Jelly
138-147	The Pipe and Glass Inn's Spiced potted Gloucester Old Spot Pork with Sticky Apple and Crackling Salad	Grilled Barnsley Lamb Chop with Devilled Kidneys, Nettle and Mint Sauce
148-157	Tuna Tartare, Red Pepper, Black Olive, Saffron Shallots, Coriander, Sour Dough Croutes	Roast Estate Pigeon, Ravioli of Woodland Mushrooms, Warm Celeriac Coleslaw
158-167	Grilled Mackerel, Handpicked Whitby Crab, Crispy Smoked Eel Boulangére Potatoes and Caper Berry Velouté	Roast "Leven Farm" Duck Breast, Fig Tart Tartin, Confit Cherries and Pear Purée
168-177	Smoked York Ham Hock Terrine, Foie Gras with Orchard Apple Chutney	Poached Halibut with Buttenut Squash Purée, King Prawn, Vanilla and Chilli Butter

DESSERTS	RESTAURANTS	PAGE
Apple Cloud, Cinnamon Cake, After Eight Flavours, Candied Apples	1885 The Restaurant	008-017
Valrhona Chocolate Tart, Popcorn and Peanut Ice Cream, Salted Caramel	Aldwark Arms	018-027
Smoked Chocolate Brownie, Pecan Parfait	Anthony's The Restaurant	028-037
Blackberry and Pistachio Crumble and Parfait	The Blue Bicycle	038-047
Chocolate, Banana, Caramel, Lime	The Burlington at The Devonshire Arms Hotel	048-057
Sticky Toffee Pudding	The Butchers Arms	058-067
Double Chocolate Cheesecake	Casa Mia Millennium	068-077
Chocolate Fondue with Marshmallows and Fruit	El Gato Negro Tapas	078-087
Lemon Meringue	Estbek House	088-097
Trio of Blackberry Desserts	The Fourth Floor Café and Bar at Harvey Nichols	098-107
Berry Meringue Cheesecake, Gin and Tonic Sorbet	The Hepworth	108-117
Spiced Carrot Cake, Cointreau and Mandarin Sorbet	Hotel du Vin & Bistro	118-127
Chocolate and Cognac Tart with Mocca Mousse. Orange Jelly and Chocolate Crisp	The Old Vicarage	128-137
Trio of Yorkshire Apples - Apple and Bramble Crumble, Sticky Apple Sponge, Apple Sorbet	The Pipe and Glass Inn	138-147
Dark Chocolate Delice, Extra Virgin Olive Oil, Hazelnuts, Milk Ice Cream	Samuel's at Swinton Park Luxury Castle Hotel	148-157
Norwood Green Strawberries and Rose Water Parfait, Sweet White Balsamic Syrup and Shortbread Biscuits	Shibden Mill Inn	158-167
Warm Berry Compote with Fraise De Bois and Lemon Thyme Ice Cream 'Canneloni'	Wentbridge House Hotel	168-177

INTRODUCTION WITH TESSA BRAMLEY

In Yorkshire we have a proud heritage of cooking and eating well; a style of cooking rooted in tradition. When I was a child, cooks celebrated seasonality and locality of food. My grandmother's skills were in making the most of the wonderful produce available on a budget: sweet white fish from the East coast, the magic of forced winter rhubarb, locally shot wild game with home-grown herbs, lamb from the hill farms, wild hedgerow fruits and foraged plants of the moors and woodlands. Her sticky spiced casseroles with wild mushrooms were legendary. As lifestyles change, so our perception of food changes, and yet, despite cooking fashions, there is a current nostalgia for proper food cooked properly.

This is a collection of local recipes from innovative Yorkshire chefs celebrating all that is best from our county. It offers a fresh, light take on traditional dishes, yet with more than a nod to the past.

Before you start, seek out the best of our local produce: that special goats' cheese only available at a certain farm gate, that fragrant wild flower honey, that plump-breasted English partridge, and then dip into these recipes and have fun – lots of fun.

Happy eating!

Tessa Bramley
The Old Vicarage

Tessa is one of Yorkshire's best known chefs and has presented TV shows for the BBC, Channel 4 and ITV, with appearances on "Here's One I Made Earlier", "Food and Drink" and "Masterchef", along with cooking slots on magazine programmes "Light Lunch" and "This Morning". She has several of her own TV series to her credit, including "Tessa Bramley's Country Kitchen", "Tessa's Seasonal Kitchen" and "Tessa's Taste Buds".

Tessa writes a regular food column for the Yorkshire Post and is a frequent contributor to national magazines and periodicals. Her first book, "The Instinctive Cook", was published in 1995, followed by "A Taste of Tradition" in 1997 and "Traditional Puddings" in 1998.

008
1885 THE RESTAURANT

The Recreation Ground, Stainland, Halifax HX4 9HF

01422 373 030
www.1885therestaurant.co.uk

Having taken the Yorkshire dining scene by storm, Nathan and Matthew Evans have cemented their reputations among Yorkshire's culinary elite. Their innovative use of the best seasonal ingredients has put 1885 The Restaurant on the map as a precedent of gastronomic dexterity. In this second edition let me tell you about what makes 1885's approach so distinctive in the catering industry. Since they first fired up the cookers and started trading they have introduced a new dynamic to their operation. They work with young people from the surrounding communities, and have established links with local catering colleges. Nathan and Matthew Evans have brought many young people from all walks of life through the 1885 ranks, training them to meet and maintain the same high standards that 1885 The Restaurant is renowned for, whilst providing them with important life skills along the way. All have gone on to forge successful careers, be it in the catering industry or otherwise.

The meticulously devised menu's change regularly and are consistently imbued with the exceptional imagination and artistry that has become the Evans Brothers' stamp. The front of house staff are as committed to their craft as Nathan and Matthew are in the kitchen and offer a personal, attentive, and friendly service. All set to the beautiful backdrop of the rolling Pennine hills, 1885 The Restaurant is truly one of the best places to enjoy the finest foods the region has to offer.

Jamie Rhodes Author and Critic

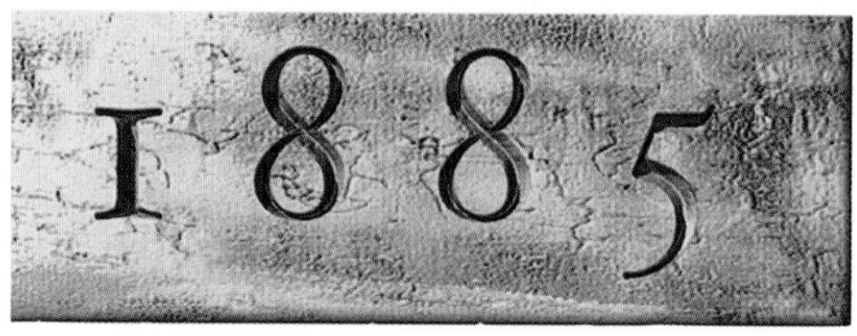

1885 photography by Tony May Images www.tonymay.com

The front of house staff are as committed to their craft as Nathan and Matthew are in the kitchen and offer a personal, attentive, and friendly service

POACHED GUINEA FOWL AND BASIL TERRINE, SLOE GIN JELLY, PICKLED SULTANAS, CONFIT ORANGE

SERVES 4

Ingredients

Guinea Fowl Terrine

4 whole guinea fowl – boned and skin removed
24 rashers bacon
1 orange – zest and segmented
20 leaves basil
500ml white wine
salt and pepper
100g caster sugar

Sloe Gin Jelly

250ml sloe gin
175g brown sugar
5 junipers
250ml white wine
6 leaves of gelatine soaked in cold water

Pickled Sultanas

250g sultanas
100g caster sugar
250ml cider vinegar
2 star anise

Confit Orange

4 oranges
100g duck fat
1 vanilla pod – deseeded

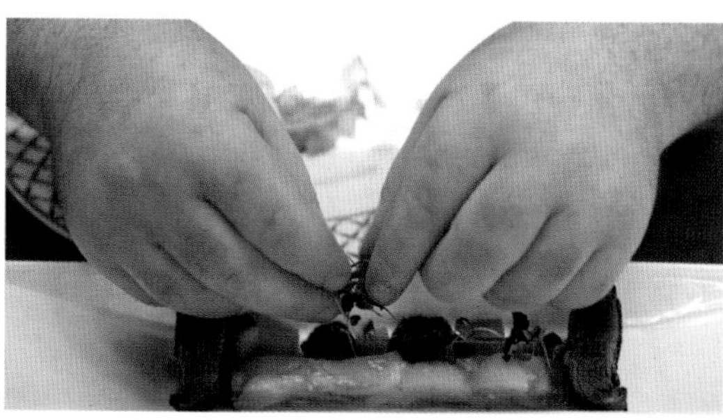

Method

For the poached guinea fowl

Take the guinea fowl of which you should have eight breasts and eight legs boned and skinned. Place in a mixing bowl, add the basil, orange zest and segments, white wine, salt and pepper and caster sugar. Mix together then cling film top and leave to marinate for at least 24 hours.

Line a desired terrine mould with a double layer of cling film (twice the size of mould) then add the bacon (make sure there is excess bacon to wrap over the top), then take the guinea fowl marinade and place in terrine mould spreading out as you do so as to get all of the different parts in the terrine. Fold in the top part of the bacon and wrap tight with the excess cling film. Bake in the oven pre heated to 180°C for 1 hour.

Place in the fridge with weights on to go cold.

For the sloe gin jelly

In a pan bring to the boil the sloe gin, brown sugar, junipers and white wine. Remove from heat and leave to infuse for 10 minutes, then reheat until boiling. Remove from heat and add the (squeezed out) gelatine. Pass into a mould to set. Leave in fridge for at least 5 hours or overnight to set. Cut into desired shape.

For the pickled sultanas

Boil sugar, vinegar and star anise. Pour over sultanas then leave in fridge to chill.

For the confit orange

Cut oranges in to quarters then slice to give little triangles. Place in bag with duck fat, vanilla seeds and pod, seal on low pressure then place in Sous vide bath on 85°C for 2 ½ hours.

To serve

Plate as seen in the picture.

VENISON LOIN AND SHOULDER, POTATO WALL, MULLED WINTER FRUITS, CHOCOLATE CANDY

SERVES 4

Ingredients

venison loin cut and trimmed

Venison Shoulder

venison shoulder
sprinkle of ginger, garlic, thyme, olive oil

Potato Wall

6 Morris Bard potatoes
cheddar cheese sauce
salt and pepper

Mulled Winter Fruits

100g sugardrop tomatoes
100g pink grapefruit
100g cherries
100g cranberries
100g apples
100g plums
250ml Mulled wine
icing sugar (as desired)

Chocolate Candy

75g clear honey
145g liquid glucose
400g caster sugar
5 tbsp of water
20g Bicarbonate soda
chocolate pistols (minimum 55% cocoa solids)

Method

For the venison loin

Cut into 5cm cylinder shapes, season and seal in a hot pan until golden brown. Place in an pre-heated oven at 175°C for 5 minutes.

For the vension shoulder

Slow cook the venison shoulder at 85°C with ginger, garlic, thyme, seasalt and olive oil for 10 hours in a sealed bag. Set the venison aside to cool then pick the meat off the shoulder bone and mix with a little olive oil. The shoulder would also be nice served with miniature raviolis (as seen on the main picture).

For the potato wall

Peel and thinly slice the potatoes then prepare a basic cheese sauce. Layer the potatoes with the cheese sauce, seasoning each layer, in a greaseproof ovenware dish. Cook at 180°C for 3 hours or until fully cooked. Leave to set in the fridge.

For the mulled wine fruit

Lightly poach the fruits in Mulled wine until bright in colour. Add a sprinkle of icing sugar if too bitter.

For the chocolate candy

Heat the honey, glucose, sugar and water together, stirring occasionally till the sugar dissolves. Increase the heat and boil the syrup until it turns a light golden caramel (152°C). Sift in the Bicarbonate of soda and then the mix will foam. Whisk this energetically for 2 minutes until the Bicarbonate of soda is dissolved into the syrup mix and the mix is light and fluffy. Pour onto a pre-lined baking tray and cool for half an hour. Turn the honeycomb over and cool for another 30 minutes then break into chunks. Melt the chocolate pistols and dip the honey comb in, leave to cool; then blitz.

To serve

Plate as seen in the picture.

APPLE CLOUD, CINNAMON CAKE, AFTER EIGHT FLAVOURS, CANDIED APPLES

SERVES 4

Ingredients

Apple Cloud

1lb sugar
1 tbsp liquid glucose
200ml fresh apple juice
2 large free-range egg whites
9 sheets gelatine soaked in 140ml apple juice
1 tsp vanilla extract

Cinnamon Cake

448g ground almonds
252g butter
192g icing sugar
8 eggs
20g ground cinnamon

After Eight Flavours

10 packs after eight

Candied Apples

10 apples (granny smith)
200ml stock syrup

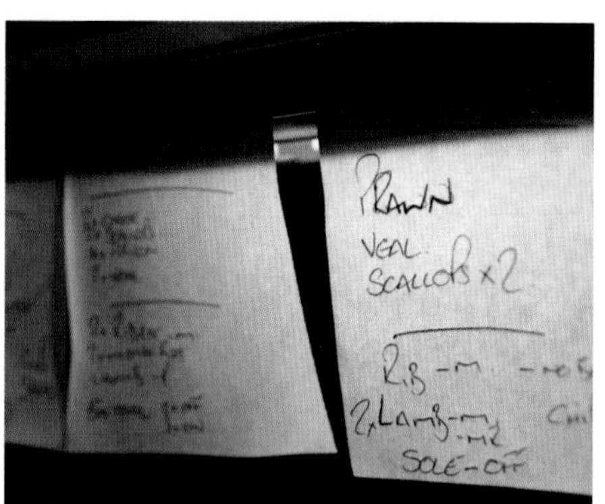

Method

For the apple cloud

Place the sugar, glucose and apple juice in a heavy-based pan. Bring to the boil and continue cooking over a high heat until it reaches 127°C/260°F on a sugar thermometer.

Meanwhile, beat the egg whites with an electric whisk until stiff peaks form when the whisk is removed.

When the syrup is up to temperature, remove from the heat and carefully slide in the softened gelatine sheets and their soaking juice. The syrup will bubble up.

Continue to beat the egg whites while slowly pouring in the hot syrup. The mixture will become shiny and start to thicken. Add the vanilla extract and continue whisking for 5-10 minutes, until the mixture is stiff and thick enough to hold its shape on the whisk.

Pour in to desired tin and leave to set up on wire rack for at least 2 hours.

For the cinnamon cake

Line tray with grease proof paper. Cream butter, sugar and cinnamon. Add ground almonds mix until smooth, add eggs, pour into tray and bake for 20-25 mins on 170°C (dry heat).

For the after eight flavours

Melt over a Bain Marie.

For the candied apples

Peel the apple then Parisienne (which means to cut out little balls), place in a vacuum bag with stock syrup, turn over excess bag and tape down to keep apples covered in liquid and poach in Sous vide machine on 56°C for 3 ½ hours. Chill before use.

To serve

Plate as seen in picture.

018 ALDWARK ARMS

Aldwark, North Yorkshire YO61 1UB

01347 838 324
www.aldwarkarms.co.uk

The Aldwark Arms is a family owned pub-restaurant in the pretty village of Aldwark around 10 miles from York and Harrogate and close to the historic market towns of Easingwold and Boroughbridge. It offers fine dining, a traditional bar, a private dining room plus outside seating and a large car park.

The restaurant is based on seasonal British food freshly prepared daily from the best locally sourced produce. Chef proprietors Chris and Nick Hill create innovative dishes using a blend of classical and modern techniques. The à la carte menu changes monthly and is supplemented by a small number of blackboard specials. You might be offered a starter of "Aldwark shoot pigeon, sous vide breast with beetroot, watercress and bacon", a main course of "50° mi-cuit" organic Isle of Bute salmon, seafood chowder with radishes and English sweet corn, roast scallop and herb buttered potatoes" or for vegetarians "Lowna Dairy goat's cheese Wellington with roast root vegetables, potato gratin and chestnuts, mulled wine jelly, marjoram and hazelnut pesto".

The carefully selected wine list offers 20 reds and 20 whites plus a good selection of sparkling and rosé with quality house wines at affordable prices. There is also a monthly Wine Tasting Dinner which is a great way to learn about different wines as well as enjoying a mouth-watering tasting menu.

In the bar you can find hand pulled beers, freshly prepared bar meals based on local Yorkshire produce as well as a good range of wines by the glass, malt whiskies and other spirits.

The roaring fire is a big attraction in the winter as is the large kitchen garden terrace for outdoor eating or drinking in the summer. Popular bar meals include "beef shin, ox tail and ale pie, mushy peas with ham hock, hand cut chips and Henderson's relish" or perhaps a "10oz Timothy Taylor's battered haddock with beef drip chips, peas and ham and "chip shop" curry sauce" followed by "sticky toffee pudding with butterscotch sauce, prune and armagnac ice cream and brandy snap".

ALDWARK
ARMS

The restaurant is based on seasonal British food freshly prepared daily from the best locally sourced produce. Chef proprietors Chris and Nick Hill create innovative dishes using a blend of classical and modern techniques

ROAST BREAST OF WOOD PIGEON WITH CRISPY LEG MEAT, BEETROOT AND DRIED FRUIT PURÉE

SERVES 4

Method

Pre heat oven to 200°C or a water bath 60°C.

For the breast of wood pigeon

Prepare the pigeons by carefully removing the legs and then salting them for 1 hour. Cook the legs very slowly in a pan of the stock until tender. Pick the meat off the pigeon legs, press them in to a small square bearing in mind you will need to cut them into 1cm square cubes.

For the beetroot purée

Peel and wash the beetroot, season and roast in the oven under tin foil until soft, then blend until smooth with the natural yoghurt.

For the dried fruit purée

Boil all the dried fruits in water until very soft and blend in a food processor with the gelatine and refrigerate.

To serve

Cut the pressed pigeon leg into small cubes and coat in breadcrumbs ready to deep fry. Seal the pigeon breasts in a hot pan, roast at 200°C for 3 minutes and rest for 5 or alternatively vacuum pack on full pressure and cook in a water bath at 60°C for 12 minutes. Warm up the beetroot purée, quenelle the dried fruit mixture and serve with the pigeon breasts and legs as seen in the picture.

Ingredients

Roast Breast of Wood Pigeon

2 whole wood pigeons
100g breadcrumbs
2 eggs
1 litre of stock (beef will be fine)

Beetroot Purée

500g fresh beetroot
200g natural yoghurt

Dried Fruit Purée

50g dried apricots
50g dried prunes
100g dried sultanas
100g dried dates
2 leaves of gelatine

ROASTED THORPE UNDERWOOD VENISON WITH A BABY SHEPHERD'S PIE, CHOCOLATE JELLY, FONDANT VEGETABLES, SAUCE CASSIS

SERVES 4

Ingredients

Venison Cuts

4 x 100g portions of venison fillet "barrel cut"steaks
1kg diced venison braising steak
1kg dry mashed potato
5 litres stock for braising
10 baking potatoes
5 very large carrots
2 swedes
500g butter
a few aromatics (thyme and garlic cloves)

For the sauce

5 litres beef stock
2kg venison bones (preferably from the saddle, chopped)
1 bottle of merlot red wine
250ml cooking Madeira
a few aromatics (thyme and garlic cloves)
100ml crème de cassis

For the chocolate jelly

40g caster sugar
2.5g agar agar
30g cocoa powder (preferably Valrhona)
400ml milk
100ml water
114g bitter chocolate (preferably Valrhona)

Method

Preheat oven to 200°C or a water bath 55°C.

For the shepherd's pie

The diced venison will need to braise slowly in the stock for several hours to make the shepherd's pie. Once the meat is cooked, put it into small cocotte serving dishes and top with the mash potato. Bake at 200°C for 20 minutes until piping hot and golden brown.

For the fondant vegetables

Dice the large carrots and swedes all the same size (approximately 2cm cubes). Cut out the potatoes with a round potato cutter. Colour the vegetables up in the butter, add some stock and aromatics and cook slowly in the oven until soft.

For the venison sauce

Roast the bones until dark brown in a hot pan. Add the roasted bones, bottle of merlot, the Madeira and the aromatics, and reduce to a glaze, then add the stock and reduce to 1 litre of liquid. Strain and add the cassis. The sauce is now ready.

For the chocolate jelly

Combine the milk and water and bring to the boil. Add the cocoa powder, sugar and agar, whisk continuously until you bring it back to the boil. Pour into a container lined with cling film and put into the fridge to set. Cut into cubes when set.

To serve

Preferably, vacuum pack the venison portions individually on full pressure and put them in a stirred water bath set at 55°C for 40 minutes. Remove from the bags and seal in a pan over high heat. To cook the venison steaks in the oven, seal them in a hot pan and cook at 200°C for 8 minutes. Carve the venison and present as shown in the picture with the shepherd's pie on the side.

VALRHONA CHOCOLATE TART, POPCORN AND PEANUT ICE CREAM, SALTED CARAMEL

SERVES 4

Ingredients

Sweet Pastry

250g plain flour
125g cold diced butter
50g caster sugar
1 egg

The Filling

250g Dark Valrhona chocolate
25g glucose
175ml cream

Peanut and Popcorn Ice Cream

100g sugar
100g pasteurized egg yolks
250ml milk
250ml cream
75g peanut butter
50g caramelised popcorn

For the Salted Caramel

1 tin of cooked carnation caramel
100ml boiling water
15g smoked Maldon sea salt

Method

For the salted caramel

Add the salt to the boiling water until dissolved and mix with the tin of carnation caramel.

For the pastry

Rub the butter into the flour, add the sugar and bind with the eggs to make the pastry, rest the pastry and then line a tart case and blind bake.

For the tart filling

Boil the cream and glucose, add the chocolate, pour into the cold tart case and set in the fridge.

For the ice cream

Boil the milk, popcorn and peanut butter, whisk together the eggs and sugar then add the cream. Cook the mix in a double boiler until it reaches 85°C, then chill and churn in an ice cream machine.

To serve

Cut the tart into four portions, serve with the salted caramel and ice cream on the side and decorate with some pieces of caramel popcorn.

028 ANTHONY'S RESTAURANT

19 Boar Lane, Leeds LS1 6EA

0113 2455 922
www.anthonysrestaurant.co.uk

Since opening its doors in 2004 Anthony Flinn has not only developed an unprecedented reputation as an expert in his field, he has also proved that he can be bold and imaginative in growing a business and a brand. From the very first day Anthony's received outstanding reviews from the most demanding food critics.

Apart from the creative and magical dishes turned out at the Boar Lane restaurant he has developed two other very impressive prime location establishments in the Corn Exchange and the Victoria Quarter both in the centre of Leeds.

Producing everything from his shops in the Corn Exchange the Bakery, Patisserie, Chocolate, Pie and Cheese shops are individual units that were developed to supply his restaurants and the retail trade with fresh produce seven days a week. As well as producing for himself he has enticed the city's top chefs to purchase many of the products he turns out. Anthony's are now supplying a plethora of local restaurants, sandwich bars and corporate businesses. Awards are not only bestowed on his fine dining restaurant he has recently won awards for his bread, cakes and chocolates.

Just like Anthony's the impressive Corn Exchange has been critically acclaimed and highly praised for being one of the best value for money establishments in Leeds without compromise to quality. His Patisserie in the Victoria Quarter sits very comfortably in the middle of the world's top brands and more than holds its own in terms of quality and style.

A man of relatively few words he speaks most eloquently through his food.

Anthony's Restaurant photography by Cris Matthews

DRESSED CRAB WITH BRAISED CHICKEN HEARTS, COCKS CREST, BASIL AND LEMON SORBET

SERVES 4

Ingredients

Dressed Crab Meat

175g fresh white crab meat
5g chopped chive
Kalamata olive oil
salt

Crispy Chicken Feet

4 chicken feet

Chicken Hearts

8 chicken hearts
braising steaks

Cocks Combs

4 cockeral combs
brasing stock
salt

Lemon and Basil Sorbet

200ml lemon juice
500g sugar
90g glucose
700ml water
10g basil

Pistachio Praline

100g pistachio oil
10ml oil

To Finish

jus
Kalamata olive oil
rocket shoots

Method

For the crab

Mix all ingredients together and store in the fridge until you are ready to serve.

For the cocks comb

Salt the comb for 12 hours. After 12 hours wash off the salt and place into your braising stock then into the oven at 110°C for 2 hours. Remove from the stock and chill fully in the fridge.

For the chicken hearts

Trim the bottom of the chicken hearts and place in the braising stock. Place in the oven at 110°C for 2 hours. Once cooked remove from the stock and store in the fridge.

For the chicken feet

Boil the feet until soft. While warm remove the bones and lay flat on grease proof paper and dry in a cool oven. Once fully dried fry in hot oil until they puff up and go crispy.

For the lemon and basil sorbet

Blanch and refresh the basil. Warm the water, glucose and sugar together until fully dissolved. Add the lemon juice. Place the mixture with the basil in a food processor and blitz. Strain through a fine sieve and churn in an ice cream machine until smooth. Store in the freezer until needed.

For the pistachio praline

Place all ingredients in to a food processor and blitz until smooth. Store in a bottle.

To serve

Place the combs and hearts in to your jus and warm. Arrange all the ingredients on the plate as shown in the picture and finish with hot jus, olive oil and the lemon sorbet.

PORK 5 WAYS

SERVES 4

Ingredients

Belly Pork

600g belly pork
1litre good braising stock

Crispy Pork Scratchings

the rind of the belly pork once cooked

Morteau Sausage

200g cooked and diced sausage

Pigs Wind Pipe

1 length of wind pipe (cut in to 4 and the centre removed)

Pigs Head Terrine

1 boiled pigs head (picked down to just meat)
10g gherkin
10g capers
10g shallot
5g chopped chives, parsley and tarragon
splash of stock
1 egg
100g bread crumbs
vegetable oil for frying

Mash Potatoes

250g potatoes
300g cream
salt

Cider Apples

1 can baby apples
½ bottle of good cider

Pearl Onions

200g butter
12 pearl onions

To Finish

jus
olive oil
cucumber ribbons

Method

For the belly pork

Place the belly in to the stock and braise in the oven for 3 hours at 110°C until cooked. Once cooked press flat in the fridge with weights.

For the pork scratchings

Remove the rind from the pork. Cut in to strips and dry in a cool oven. Once dried fully fry in hot oil until they triple in size. Finish with salt.

For the pearl onions

Peel the onions and place in a small saucepan. Add the butter and a splash of water and cook on a low heat until soft.

For the mash

Boil the potatoes until cooked. Reduce the cream by two thirds. Mash the potatoes and fold in whilst hot.

For the pigs head terrine

Mix all the ingredients together and press in a terrine mould. Chill in the fridge. Once set cut in to 1 inch squares. Coat the squares in the egg and bread crumbs and store until you are ready to serve.

For the cider apples

Place the apples in to a vacuum pouch and cover with the cider. Vac pack the apple and leave to absorb the cider. The longer you leave it the better they are.

For the pistachio praline

Place all ingredients in to a food processor and blitz until smooth. Store in a bottle.

To serve

Cut the belly pork in to 4 pieces, pan roast the side and place in the oven. Place the wind pipe and the sausage in the jus and bring to the boil. Fry the terrine in the oil and season. Lay the cucumber out and cut to a square. Lay on the plate. Pipe the mash in to the centre of the wind pipe. Arrange the items on the plate as shown in the picture. Finish with the sausage and jus and dress with the oil.

SMOKED CHOCOLATE BROWNIE, PECAN PARFAIT

SERVES 4

Ingredients

Brownie

185g flour
3 large eggs
40g cocoa
275g sugar
60g pecans
185g butter
wood chips

Chocolate Caramel

100g glucose
100g sugar
20g cocoa powder

Black Treacle Ice Cream

200ml cream
300ml milk
5 egg yolks
40g black treacle

Pecan Parfait

200ml double cream
3 egg yolks
2 leaves of gelatine
60g sugar
200g mascarpone cheese
200g chopped toasted pecans

Toffee Sauce

100ml double cream
100ml sugar

Chocolate and Sea Salt Fudge

500g milk chocolate
1 tin of condensed milk
sea salt
chopped pecan nuts

Method

For the brownie

Cream the sugar and eggs together. Melt the chocolate. Beat the flour and cocoa into the eggs until smooth. Fold in melted chocolate and mix until fully incorporated. Fold in the pecans. Spread the mixture in a tray and bake in the oven at 180°C for 25-30 minutes. Once cooked chill in the fridge. When the brownie is cool, cut into the desired shape and place on a wire rack. Sprinkle the wood chips into a heavy bottomed tray and place on the stove. Once they begin to smoke place the wire rack and brownies in the tray and tin foil the top. Smoke for 4 minutes. Remove the brownies and store until ready to serve.

For the chocolate caramel

Place all ingredients in to a pan. Boil the sugars to 160°C then add the cocoa stirring quickly. Pour on to a heat proof mat and allow to cool.

For the treacle ice cream

Bring the milk and cream to the boil. Cream the yolks and treacle together. Pour the hot cream over the egg mix whilst whisking. Return to the heat and cook until it coats the back of a spoon. Stir continuously. Chill in the fridge. Once cold churn in the ice cream machine. Store in the freezer.

For the pecan parfait

First soak the gelatine in cold water. Whisk the sugar and egg yolks together until white. Bring the cream to the boil and pour over the eggs while whisking then add the soaked gelatine. Chill in the fridge. Once the mixture is cold whisk in a machine with the mascarpone and pecans until ribbon stage. Make a tube from acetate and close one end with cling film. Pipe mixture in to the tube and store in the freezer.

For the toffee sauce

Boil the sugar and cream together until golden brown. Chill in a bottle in the fridge.

For the chocolate fudge

Melt the chocolate and place in a mixing bowl. Whisk the condensed milk in to the chocolate until fully incorporated. Pour in to a tray and set in the fridge. Once set, cut into the desired shape and sprinkle with cocoa and sea salt.

To serve

Place caramel in the oven between two heat proof mats. Once soft roll thinly with a rolling pin. Remove the top mat and with your fingers pull the caramel in to long strands. Allow to cool. Place brownie on the plate. Remove the plastic from around the parfait and roll in the chopped nuts. Finish with dots of toffee sauce and sea salt.

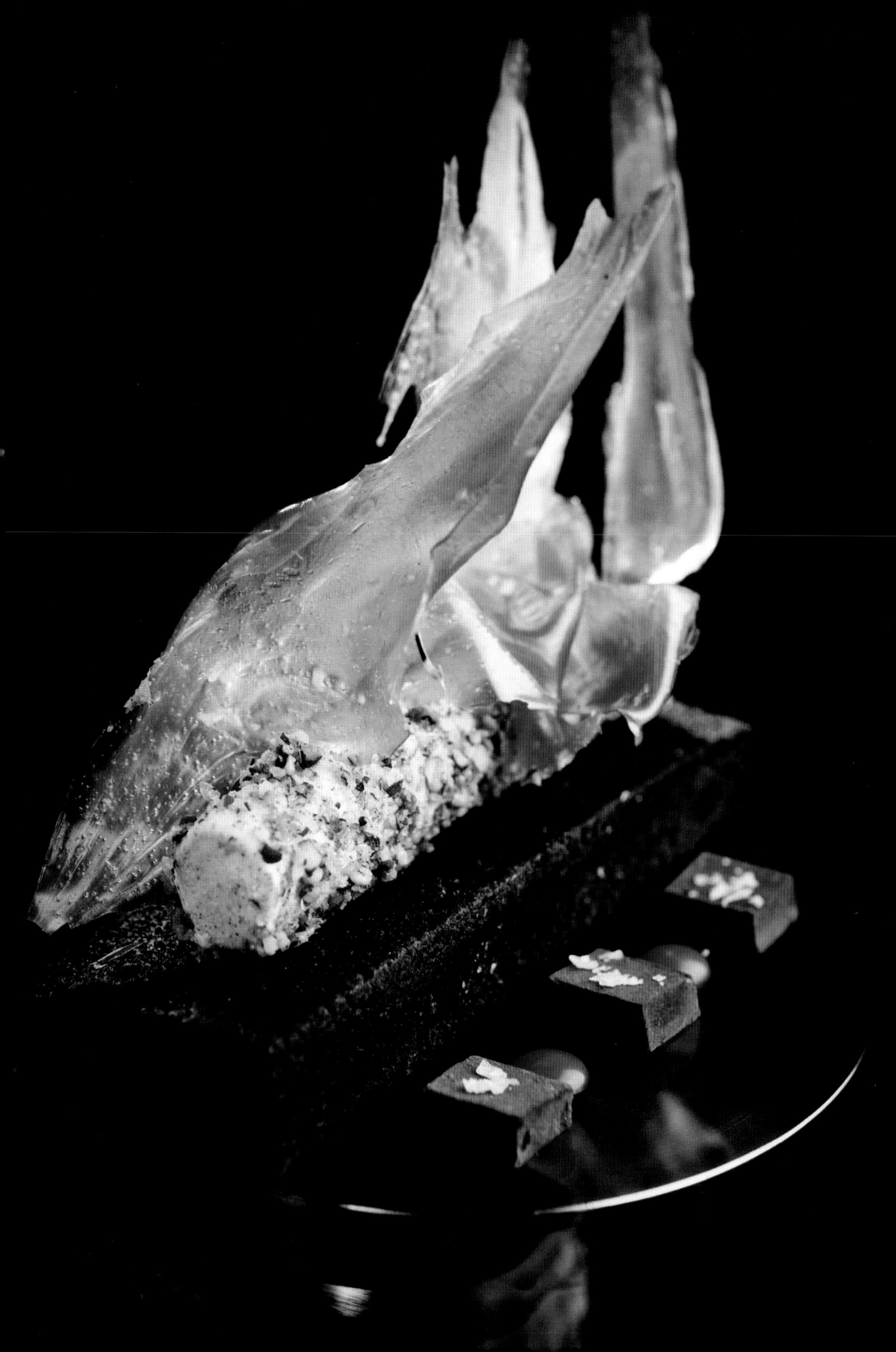

038 THE BLUE BICYCLE

34 Fossgate, York YO1 9TA

01904 673 990
www.thebluebicycle.com

Based in the centre of York, The Blue Bicycle is one of the city's most talked about restaurants, where we serve award-winning food in a relaxed dining atmosphere. We are highly commended for our fresh fish dishes, homemade desserts and for our extensive selection of fine wines.
At the turn of the century our cellar was a brothel of some repute. In fact if you wander downstairs, you will see photographs of some of the girls, who perhaps, plied their ware.
We now serve romantic dinners in the private vaulted booths (or beds), which are situated in the opulent and atmospheric dining area. You can enjoy a pre-dinner tipple overlooking the River Foss, reflecting on this bygone era of impropriety. The upstairs dining area exudes warmth and a busy atmosphere, with an eclectic range of tables and chairs, all beautifully presented. Lunch or Dinner with us is a high quality dining experience in exemplary surroundings, set in an intriguingly historic building, even by York's standards. We are totally committed to your comfort and relaxation and we pride ourselves on courteous attention to detail, a friendly approach and flexibility of service. We use the freshest ingredients, prepared and presented to the highest standards.

Situated alongside the River Foss we also offer beautiful modern rooms. The Blue Rooms are luxurious, convenient, private and comfortable – perfect for leisure or business visitors or that short romantic break. The rooms have a cool minimalist feel with tasteful contemporary interiors. Our wish is to ensure that the time spent with us is truly enjoyable and memorable, whether it is for a meal in our restaurant or a stay in the Blue Rooms.

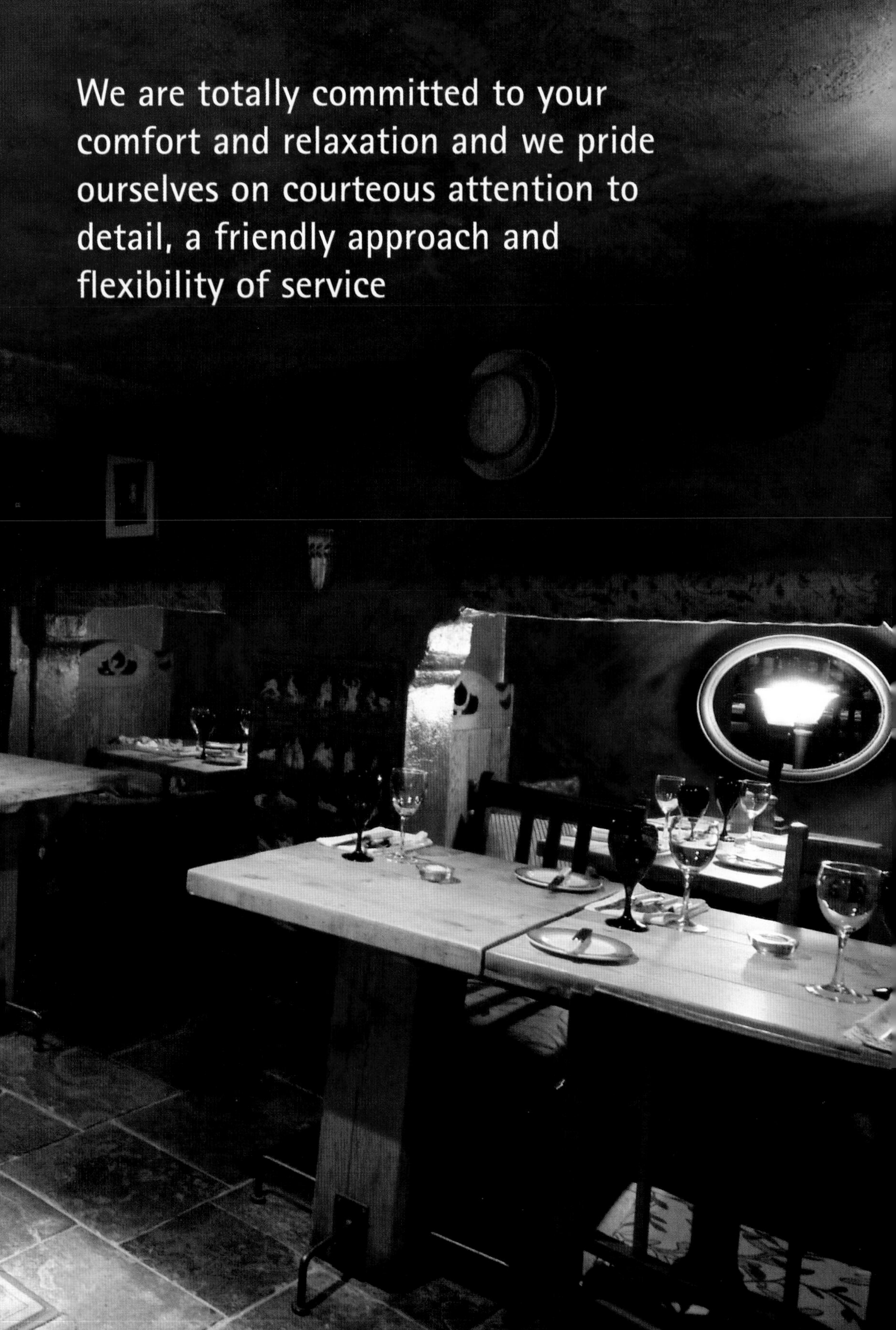
We are totally committed to your comfort and relaxation and we pride ourselves on courteous attention to detail, a friendly approach and flexibility of service

PAN SEARED SCALLOPS WITH SPICED AUBERGINE, CHESTNUT PURÉE AND SALTED HAZELNUTS

SERVES 4

Ingredients

Scallops

3 scallops per person
splash of any type of oil
a knob of butter to finish

Spiced Aubergine

1 aubergine
splash of any type of oil
salt and pepper
1/4 tsp cayenne pepper
1/4 tsp Cardamom
1/4 tsp hot curry powder
1/4 tsp Chinese five spice

Chestnut Purée

300g cooked peeled chestnuts
100g butter
200ml double cream
salt and pepper

Salted Hazelnuts

5 peeled hazelnuts per person
splash of any type of oil
salt

Method

For the chestnut purée

Bring to the boil the butter, cream and chestnuts, simmer for 1 minute and remove from the heat. Purée with a hand blender and season to taste as required.

For the spiced aubergine

Cut the aubergine into 8 pieces lengthways, oil and dust with spices (do this about an hour before serving to allow the aubergine to take on spices). When needed grill until soft and golden.

For the scallops

In a hot frying pan add a little oil and butter, then carefully place scallops in the pan and leave for about 45 seconds to 1 minute. Lift one and if it is starting to crust turn over and repeat with others. (Scallops can be cooked as little or as long as personally required according to taste).

For the salted hazelnuts

Place peeled hazelnuts in a bowl. Add oil and season with table salt. Use as needed.

To serve

Assemble as seen in picture

PAN FRIED FILLET OF EAST COAST COD WITH A GOATS CHEESE CRUST, LEMON THYME MASH, WATERCRESS BEIGNET AND ROAST TOMATO OIL

SERVES 4

Ingredients

4 cod fillets (250g each)
sunflower, vegetable or olive oil (for cooking only)

Goats Cheese Crust

200g goats cheese
200g breadcrumbs
150g butter
salt and pepper

Lemon Thyme Mash

1kg red skin potatoes
200g butter
10 sprigs lemon thyme
salt and pepper

Watercress Beignet

1 punnet watercress
4 eggs
120ml milk
100g butter
140g plain flour

Roast Tomato Oil

5 tomatoes
5tsp tomato purée
1 clove garlic
100ml olive oil

Method

For the goats cheese crust

Place the breadcrumbs and goats cheese in a blender with a pinch of salt and pepper and blend. Melt the butter and add to the ingredients and blend further. Roll out the crust between 2 pieces of greaseproof paper, place in fridge for 1 hour. Once the crust has set, cut into a shape according to size of the cod.

For the beignet

Using a hand blender, blend the milk and watercress. Then in a pan bring to boil the milk and watercress mixture and the butter. Add the sifted flour and stir until the mixture comes away from the side of the pan. Remove from the heat. Transfer to a separate dish and add eggs one at a time until it becomes a smooth paste. Add salt and pepper and allow to cool. Teaspoon the mix into a hot fryer (at 200°C) for about 3 minutes until dark golden brown.

For the lemon thyme mash

Peel the potatoes, boil and mash and leave to cool. Melt the butter and add the picked thyme, then add the mash and stir until hot and the mash becomes silky and comes away from the sides of the pan.

For the roast tomato oil

Roast the tomatoes and garlic for 15 minutes at 210°C, place in a blender with the oil and tomato purée, taste and season as required.

For the cod

In an oiled frying pan on a medium heat, place cod skin side down and seal for about 1 minute. Remove cod from pan and place on a baking tray. Place the crust on the skin side up and bake at 200°C for 10 minutes.

To serve

Assemble as seen on picture.

BLACKBERRY AND PISTACHIO CRUMBLE AND PARFAIT

SERVES 4

Ingredients

Blackberry Parfait

150g caster sugar
45g water
5 egg yolks
250ml whipped cream
200g blitzed blackberries

Pistachio Parfait

as per Blackberry Parfait, but exchange blackberries for pistachio nuts

Crumble Topping

50g pistachio nuts
20g almonds
20g peanuts
20g walnuts
20g hazelnuts
100g brown sugar
50g caster sugar
200g butter
10g nutmeg

Blackberry Crumble Filling

500g blackberries
100g pistachio nuts
1 vanilla pod (scraped)
200g caster sugar

Crème Anglaise

200ml double cream
200ml milk
1 vanilla pod
200g sugar
8 egg yolks

Method

For the blackberry parfait

Whisk egg yolks until pale. Boil sugar and water to 118°C. Whisk together and leave until cool. Whip cream to a firm consistency. Add the blitzed blackberries to the cream and fold into the cold egg and sugar mix.

For the pistachio parfait

As per blackberry parfait, but exchange blackberries for pistachio nuts. Put both cool parfait mixes in a tray and leave in the freezer for 6 hours.

For the crumble topping

Toast all of the nuts and blitz with a hand blender or food processor. Crumb the sugar and butter together. Add the toasted nuts to the sugar and butter mix. Bake on a flat tray for 20 minutes at 180°C.

For the crumble filling

Cook blackberries, sugar, pistachio nuts and vanilla pod on a medium heat to soften.

For the crème anglaise

Put the milk and cream on to heat. Whisk eggs, sugar and vanilla. Add hot milk and cream to eggs and sugar. Cook on the stove until the mixture coats the back of the spoon.

To serve

Assemble as seen in picture.

048 THE BURLINGTON

The Devonshire Arms Country House Hotel and Spa, Bolton Abbey, Near Skipton, North Yorkshire BD23 6AJ

01756 710 441
www.thedevonshirearms.co.uk
www.devonshirechefs.co.uk

As the most highly rated restaurant in Yorkshire, with 4 AA Rosettes and a Michelin star; the Burlington is renowned for outstanding award-winning food, accompanied by one of the most remarkable wine lists in the country. A haven for complete relaxation and outstanding hospitality, the hotel is in a parkland setting on The Duke of Devonshire's 30,000 acre estate and surrounded by the glorious scenery of Wharfedale. The historic hotel has evolved over the centuries to provide today's guest with contemporary comforts in an atmosphere of grace and charm with supremely comfortable bedrooms and a choice of two restaurants - the celebrated Burlington, named after an ancestor of The Duke of Devonshire, and the vibrant Devonshire Brasserie and Bar. At the helm of the Burlington is Steve Smith, a leading light of the northern cooking scene for more than fifteen years and over ten of those years with a Michelin star to his name. Calm, modest and thoroughly professional Steve produces groundbreaking food in a style that is both visually exciting and a thrill for the tastebuds. Totally passionate about his craft, from good shopping for the best fresh seasonal produce to the final performance when guests are blown away by an exceptional imagination and artistry, the end result firmly benchmarks Steve, as one of the country's top chefs. And whilst chefs' reputations may be built on stars and awards, of which Steve has notched up his fair share, he says, "What really matters is that my diners enjoy a fantastic meal and want to return again and again." And they do.

PRODUCE
CHATEAU PICHON LONGUEVILLE
COMTESSE DE LALANDE
OF FRANCE
GRAND CRU CLASSE
1982
PAUILLAC
APPELLATION PAUILLAC CONTROLEE
MIS EN BOUTEILLE AU CHATEAU
1990

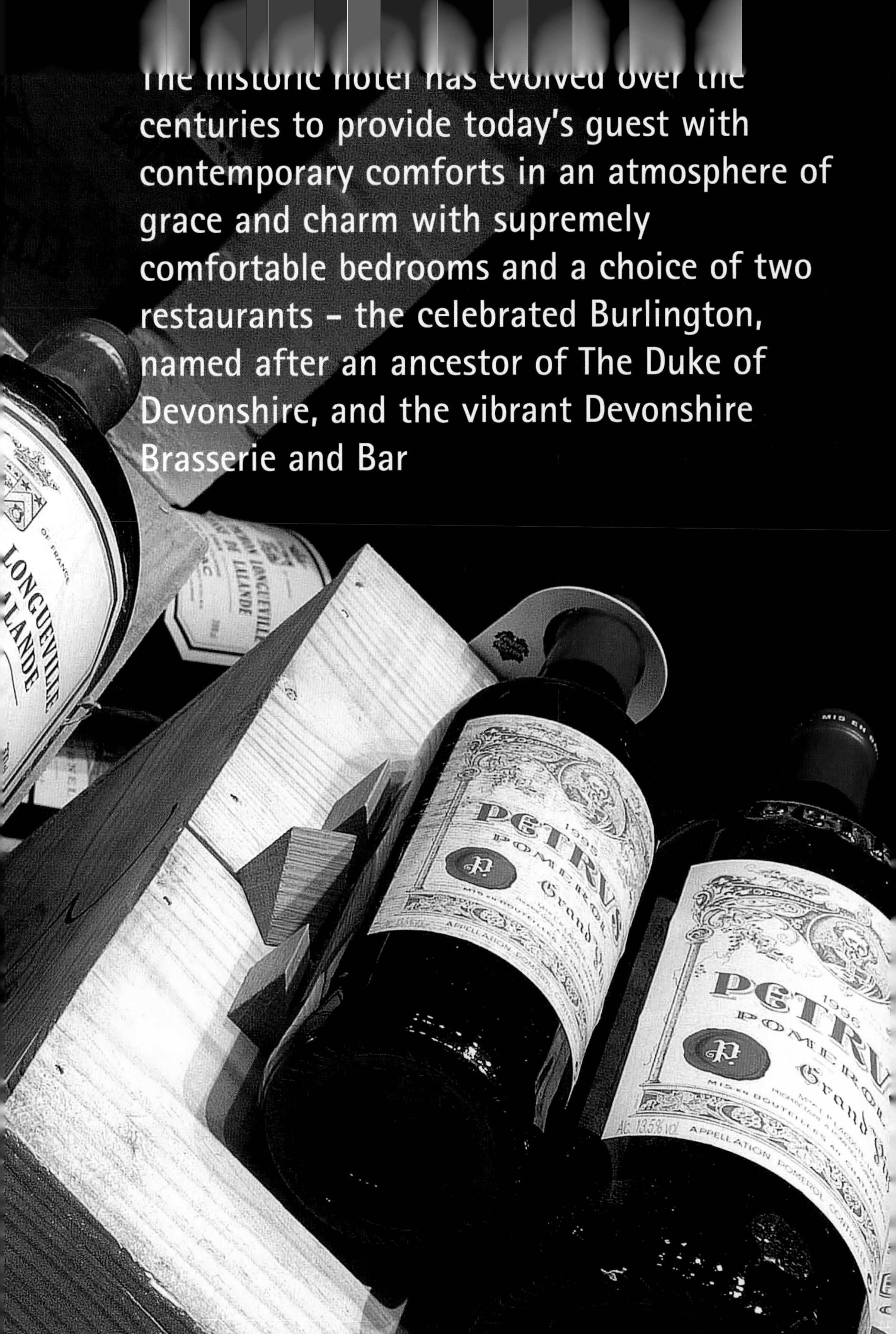

The historic hotel has evolved over the centuries to provide today's guest with contemporary comforts in an atmosphere of grace and charm with supremely comfortable bedrooms and a choice of two restaurants – the celebrated Burlington, named after an ancestor of The Duke of Devonshire, and the vibrant Devonshire Brasserie and Bar

SEARED SCALLOP, CELERIAC, APPLE, SMOKED EEL, TRUFFLE

SERVES 8

Ingredients

2 scallops per portion
3 pieces smoked eel per person (cut into 1cm x 1cm cubes)
sliced apple (thinly sliced)
celery cress
sliced truffle (thinly sliced)

Celeriac Purée

1 head of celeriac
splash of milk
splash of cream
1 tsp celery salt
1 tsp truffle oil
25g truffle (grated)

Apple Jelly

450ml Cawston apple juice
25g vegetable gelatine

Truffle Vinaigrette

50ml truffle oil
50ml 12 year old balsamic vinegar (wild harvest)
50ml pommace oil

Method

For the celeriac purée

Peel and finely chop the celeriac. Place into a saucepan, cover with milk and cream, then add the salt.

Bring to the boil and simmer until soft.

Drain the liquid using a sieve, and then blend the remaining mixture until completely smooth.

Finally, add the truffle oil and truffle, re-blend and store in the fridge.

For the apple jelly

Bring 250ml of the apple juice to the boil and reduce until about 50ml remains.

Whisk the vegetable gelatine into the remaining 200ml of juice.

Add the two juice mixes together in a pan, bring back to the boil and pour into a jelly mould.

Allow to set and cut as required.

For the truffle vinaigrette

Blend all the ingredients together then transfer to a squeezy bottle.

To serve

Pan-fry the scallops for approximately 2 minutes on each side.

Place a spoonful of the purée at the side of the plate, then place the eel, apple, celery cress and sliced truffle around the plate.

Place two scallops next to each other on the plate and drizzle with the vinaigrette.

LAMB TEXTURES

SERVES 6

Ingredients

1 loin of lamb

Stock

75ml white wine
1 sprig of rosemary
2 cloves of garlic
1 celery stick
½ onion
1 tomato

Tomatoes

16 San Marzano tomatoes
1 tbsp olive oil
1 clove garlic finely sliced
sprig thyme
pinch of salt
pinch of sugar

Broccoli Purée

2 heads of broccoli (approximately 500g)
250g of double cream
½ garlic clove
salt

Sauce

lamb stock
50ml Noilly Prat vermouth
1 tomato chopped
the juice from ½ lemon
½ sprig rosemary

Method

For the lamb

Sear the lamb loin in a hot pan until the fat has caramelised, then roast in a hot oven to your liking.

For the stock

Pour the white wine into the same pan in which you seared the lamb, using a wooden spoon to remove as much of the caramelised meat juices as possible. Pour through a small tea strainer and keep to one side. Add the celery, onion and tomato to a different pan and cook until golden. Drain in a colander to remove excess fat or oil. Then add these to the pan with the white wine, rosemary and garlic. Simmer for 30 minutes, skimming off any impurities that collect at the top of the pan. Pass the stock through a chinois (fine mesh sieve) and then through double muslin twice. Finally, return to the boil and reduce by half.

For the sauce

Place the stock, Noilly Prat and tomato into a pan and bring to the boil. Skim any impurities from the top if required. Add the rosemary and garlic, then reduce by half. Pass sauce through a piece of muslin and return to the pan. Season with salt and lemon juice if required. Just before serving monte (melt) a little butter into the sauce.

For the broccoli purée

Separate the florets from the broccoli, then juice the stalks using a juicing machine. Bring the garlic and cream to the boil and leave to infuse while cooling. Bring a pan of seasoned water to the boil and cook the broccoli florets for approximately 10 minutes. Refresh immediately in iced water. Remove from ice and allow all the water to drain. Place the cream mix, broccoli florets and some of the reserved juice into a blender and blend to a smooth purée. Add more broccoli juice if required. Season to taste. Pass through a fine chinois, then cover with cling film and store as required.

For the tomatoes

Blanch and peel the tomatoes. Mix together with all other ingredients and place on a tray in a hot cupboard for 8 hours to dry out.

To serve

Re-heat the purée and spoon to one side of the plate, then arrange the tomatoes around the edge of the plate. Slice the lamb and arrange next to the purée. Pour the sauce into a sauce boat to be served at the table. In the Burlington, we serve this dish with home-made gnocchi.

CHOCOLATE, BANANA, CARAMEL, LIME

SERVES 8

Ingredients

Liquid Chocolate Base

125g 70% Valhrona chocolate (chopped)
125g 40% Valhrona chocolate (chopped)
250ml cream
30ml milk
10g honey
1 vanilla pod
2g smoked salt
1 gelatine leaf (soaked)

Banana Purée

200g banana juice
10g multidextrin
1 gallan gum
15g sugar

Lime Sorbet

400ml fresh lime juice
150g dextrose
100g sugar
60ml water
4 lime leaves
zest of 2 limes, microplane

Caramel Powder

100g sugar
20ml water
80g unsalted butter
15g Maldon smoked salt
75ml double cream
105g salted caramel
95g tapioca flour

Bitter Toffee Sauce

100g sugar
25g glucose
40ml milk
4g xanthium gum
20g butter
15g Angostura bitter

Method

For the liquid chocolate base

Place the milk, cream and vanilla in a pan and bring to the boil, add the gelatine, honey and salt and whisk in.

Pour the liquid over the chocolate and, when melted, whisk together.

Allow to cool slightly, then pour into a frame and freeze.

For the banana purée

Place ingredients into a thermomix and heat to 90°C. Reduce the temperature to 37°C.

For the lime sorbet

Place the water, dextrose, sugar, and lime leaves in a pan and bring to the boil.

Remove from the heat and add the lime zest. Allow to cool.

Stir in the lime juice and pass through a chinois (fine sieve). Place in a paco jet beaker (similar to an ice cream maker) and freeze. Churn when required.

For the salted caramel

In a heavy bottomed pan, heat the sugar and water until it turns to a caramel, then add the double cream.

Add the butter to the mix slowly. Finally add the salt and warm the mixture to ensure it has dissolved.

Pass through a chinois and store.

For the caramel powder

Whisk the tapioca flour and multidextrin into the caramel. It will eventually turn into a powder.

For the bitter toffee sauce

In a heavy bottomed pan, heat the sugar and glucose until it turns to a light caramel.

Add the milk then allow to cool slightly.

Place into a blender and gradually add the butter. Finally add the gum powder and Angostura bitter.

To serve

Place the chocolate base in the centre of the plate, put a spoonful of caramel powder on top, then place a spoonful of the sorbet on top of this.

Arrange the toffee sauce and banana purée around the plate, admire and enjoy!

058 THE BUTCHERS ARMS

38 Towngate Hepworth, Holmfirth, Huddersfield HN9 1TE

01484 682 361
www.thebutchersarmshepworth.co.uk

Since taking over The Butchers Arms in 2008, renowned Yorkshire chef Timothy Bilton has transformed it into a vibrant, award-winning dining pub which has not only become a focal point for village life, but also attracts diners from far and wide. The restaurant serves classic British food with a modern twist, making the most of the fabulous local produce, Timothy operates a unique sourcing policy of only using ingredients that are produced within a 75 mile radius of Hepworth. The result is a menu bursting with fabulous food that's all Yorkshire grown or made. Timothy has also introduced some quirky touches, such as his famous Yorkshire Tapas - a local take on the Spanish original! The pub has become particularly renowned for its spectacular Sunday lunches. Whatever is on the menu, Timothy's passion for seasonality and sustainability is always a key factor in the dishes on offer.

With crackling fires and cosy armchairs, a warm welcome awaits during the colder months, whilst in the summer a 'secret garden' offers stylish alfresco dining. The Butchers Arms is now one of West Yorkshire's most successful eateries, winning a clutch of recent awards including Yorkshire Life's 'Dining Pub of the Year 2009', plus 'Best Use of Regional Produce on the Menu' at the deliciouslyorkshire Awards and 'Best Gastropub' at the Great British Pub Awards in 2010.

Timothy Bilton has lived and breathed food all his life, training under Raymond Blanc at Le Manoir aux Quat' Saisons before working in France. Returning to Yorkshire, he was headhunted to become head chef at Bibi's Italian Restaurant in Leeds before taking over The Butchers Arms. He is now also much in demand for cookery demonstrations and festivals all over Yorkshire, and for two years running has been invited to participate in the BBC TV show Great British Menu.

THE
Cup of Olives
Warm Bread &
Butchers Arms
Large shell on King
King Scallops,
Smoked Venison
Bresola, Rocket
1/2 dozen No.1
10oz Ribeye flamed in
8oz Fillet topped with
The Butchers Arms
Pan Seared Calves
with a white
Venison Osso Bucco
Whole grilled lemon
golden
WATER

With crackling fires and cosy armchairs, a warm welcome awaits during the colder months, whilst in the summer a 'secret garden' offers stylish alfresco dining

SMOKING VENISON CARPACCIO

SERVES 4

Method

Season the venison loin, then sear in a hot pan and place into a preheated oven for 3-4 mins.

Roll the cooked venison in the chopped herbs, wrap tightly in cling film and leave to cool.

To smoke

Place the venison under the glass dome and inject smoke underneath until the dome is full.

Leave for 7 minutes, carve the venison into 20 thin slices.

To serve

Place 5 slices onto each plate and assemble the salad with crushed hazelnuts and micro herbs and garnish with parmesan shavings, beetroot reduction and smoked oil.

Ingredients

250g venison loin
1 sprig rosemary
1 sprig thyme
100g chopped parsley
250g mixed baby leaf salad
50g crushed hazelnuts
50g parmesan shavings
apple wood smoking chips

To Garnish

beetroot reduction
smoked oil
micro herbs

PLATE OF PIG

SERVES 4

Ingredients

1 pork fillet (250g)
1 pork belly (400g)
2 litres duck fat
4 slices smoked streaky bacon
5 apples (peeled and cored)
50g butter
100g sugar
250g black pudding
4 cheese and chive sausages
2 shallots (finely sliced rings)
8 large sage leaves (deep fried)
4 slices Parma ham (dried out)

200ml base sauce

Cassoulet

1 carrot
1 onion
1 leek
1 stick of celery
100ml pork stock
100g haricot beans soaked and cooked
250g chopped tomatoes
sprig rosemary
sprig thyme
tbsp garlic purée
100g diced chorizo

Method

For the pork fillet

Cut the Pork fillet into four, wrap each piece in a rasher of bacon, seal in a hot pan and finish in the oven for 12 minutes.

For the pork belly

Cover the pork belly in duck fat, cover with greaseproof paper and tin foil and cook in the oven for 2½ hours at gas mark 2. Remove from the fat and press with weight until cool, once cooled and flat cut into four pieces.

For the sausages

Cook sausage and black pudding in the oven for 12 minutes. Crisp the top of the belly pork in a hot pan and warm through with the pork fillet.

For the cassoulet

Sweat the veg, garlic and chorizo, add chopped tomatoes and haricot beans and 100ml water and bring to boil with the rosemary and thyme, season to taste and serve alongside.

For the apple sauce

Peel and core the apples, sweat down with butter and sugar until soft.

To serve

Flour and deep fry the shallot rings, deep fry the sage leaves and dry out the Parma ham.

Assemble as in the picture and finish with base sauce.

STICKY TOFFEE PUDDING

SERVES 4

Method

For the toffee pudding

Cream butter and sugar until smooth, add egg and mix well. Add flour and baking powder.

Soak dates in the boiling water with the bicarb, when soft and add to the butter mixture.

Bake in a greased and floured baking tin for 40-45 minutes at 180°C or until firm.

Cut into four pieces.

For the sauce

Heat all ingredients in a pan and bring to the boil, serve in a jug alongside the pudding.

To serve

Garnish as in the picture with mint, ice cream, clotted cream, red currants and icing sugar.

Ingredients

Toffee Pudding

150g light brown sugar
50g butter
200g self raising flour
1tsp baking powder
150g chopped dates
½ pint boiling water
1 tsp Bicarbonate of soda
1 egg

Sauce

100ml double cream
40g butter
40g dark brown sugar

Garnish

4 sprigs mint
4 brandy snaps
300g caramel ice cream
100g clotted cream
1 punnet red currants
icing sugar

068 CASA MIA MILLENNIUM

Millennium Square, Leeds LS2 3AD

0113 245 4121
www.casamiaonline.com

Leeds based Casa Mia, is a family run Italian restaurant business, with sites both in the city centre and in the nearby suburb of Chapel Allerton.
Francesco and Marta Mazzella opened their first Casa Mia restaurant in Chapel Allerton, and Casa Mia grew from there, quickly gaining a loyal and regular customer base, hungry for all the delights that they have to offer.
Priding itself on offering fresh, quality, homemade Italian cuisine,
Casa Mia provides its customers with the real taste of Italy, and whichever restaurant you visit, you will be sure of a warm welcome, and an authentic Italian atmosphere. Casa Mia offers A La Carte dining, along with special set menus - confidently catering for large party bookings, with private dining facilities also available.
Casa Mia has a fantastic special events calendar, including monthly cookery classes, and indulgent gourmet wine evenings. They have also expanded into a successful outside catering business, offering delicious Italian cuisine for all events from small business lunches to large wedding events, and everything in between.
Casa Mia recently launched a takeaway delivery service, bringing restaurant quality food, at takeaway prices, right to its customers doors! Casa Mia has won numerous awards including Best Al Fresco restaurant 2008, Best Family Restaurant 2009, Best Italian Restaurant 2010 and Best Breakfast 2010.

Nobile

Casa Mia provides its customers with the real taste of Italy, and whichever restaurant you visit, you will be sure of a warm welcome, and an authentic Italian atmosphere

Minestrone Parmiggiana di Melenzane Amarena Valpolicella
Deliziosa

KING PRAWNS

SERVES 4

Ingredients

28 raw peeled king prawns
2 cloves of garlic
5g ginger
splash white wine
20ml veg stock
olive oil

Garnish

4 courgette
4 carrots
2 red peppers

Method

For the prawns

Heat frying pan with the olive oil, when oil is hot add the prawns, brown on first side, turn over the prawns and add the garlic and ginger, cook for 1 minute.

Remove the prawns and keep warm, add the wine and stock and cook for a further minute.

Add the extra virgin olive oil and the sauce will thicken slightly.

Season with salt and pepper.

For the garnish

Slice courgettes finely with a mandolin, followed by the carrots. Next blanch in boiling water for 2 minutes. Refresh. Roll courgette and carrot into a circle (with courgette on the outside) and trim any uneven edges. Roast red peppers for 10-15 minutes and peel off the skin. To make them into circles, cut out circle shape using a ring cutter.

To serve

Pour the sauce over the prawns and add the garnish as seen in picture. Serve immediately.

GUANCIA DI BUE BRASATA

SERVES 4

Ingredients

4 ox cheeks
2 sticks celery
1 onion
2 carrots
2 bay leaf
2 cloves of garlic
200ml red wine
200ml beef stock
salt and pepper

Carrot Purée

6 carrots
20g butter
salt and pepper

Method

For the ox cheeks

Firstly remove the fat and sinus from the top of the ox cheek, do not remove the sinus from inside because that is what keeps it moist.

When they are clean heat an oven proof dish, add oil and wait for it to become really hot.

Dust the cheeks in seasoned flour and fry until golden brown on all sides.

Remove cheeks and put to one side, then fry the vegetables in the same pan until they have some colour.

Add the cheeks back to the pan, on top of the vegetables; they will act as a base to protect the cheeks.

Pour in the wine and stock, and cover with aluminium foil and the lid. Cook for 5 hours on a low heat of 150°C.

Remove from oven after this time and gently take the cheeks out from the liquid, strain the vegetables and reduce the sauce by two thirds.

For the carrot purée

Peel and chop 6 carrots. Put onto boil with 100g of butter, vegetable stock and enough water to cover carrots. Bring to the boil then turn down the heat and cook until all liquid has gone (this should roughly take 15-18 minutes). Add the carrots to a blender and blitz till smooth. Push purée through a sieve and season with salt and pepper.

To serve

Serve with carrot purée and the reduced sauce liquor.

DOUBLE CHOCOLATE CHEESECAKE

SERVES 12

Ingredients

White Layer of Cheesecake

250ml double cream
125ml cream cheese
50g sugar
100g white chocolate
7.5g gelatine

Black Layer of Cheesecake

250ml double cream
125ml cream cheese
50g sugar
125g dark chocolate
8.5g gelatine

The Base

225g digestive biscuits
50g butter

Method

For the base

Crush the biscuits in a food processor (or put them in a plastic bag and bash with a rolling pin).

Mix with the butter.

Press the mixture into 12 rings of 6cm diameter and chill.

For the chocolate mixes

Use 2 separate bowls.

Add the cheese to the sugar, heat the cream in a pan then add the gelatine (be careful not to over heat).

Melt the chocolate in a microwave or use a glass bowl set over a pan of simmering water.

Fold the cream, sugar and chocolate together and leave to cool for a couple of minutes. Then fill the rings up to half of the ring.

Repeat the same steps with the other chocolate ingredients then chill.

To serve

As seen in picture

078 EL GATO NEGRO TAPAS

Oldham Road, Ripponden, Sowerby Bridge HX6 4DN

01422 823 070
www.elgatonegrotapas.co.uk

You don't need Barcelona for the buzz or the flavours of a great Tapas Bar, there' s one right in the heart of Ripponden, West Yorkshire. Talented chef-owner Simon Shaw left a successful career with Harvey Nichol's in London to return North to open the Spanish style restaurant which quickly gained both a regional and national reputation for its fresh, lively and competent cooking. On most nights the place is buzzing and were it not for the Yorkshire stone floors, beamed ceilings and skilled local staff, it is hard to not believe this is a Spanish bar.
The food is prepared from ingredients both imported directly from Spain and sourced locally. From authentic Spanish meats, hams, and cheeses, fresh fish and seafood through to pillow-soft garlicky Catalan bread, fat olives and delicious oils, the menu caters for all tastes and diets. Eat as much or as little as you like through the novel paper menu ordering system - read the menu, tick the box next to whichever tapas dish takes your fancy and sit back as the food arrives from the kitchen in a steady flow.
Check on price deals on food and wine for midweek dinners and weekend lunches.

OLDHAM ROAD
ELGATO NEG
ELGATO NEGRO TAPAS
01422 823 070

On most nights the place is buzzing and were it not for the Yorkshire stone floors, beamed ceilings and skilled local staff, it is hard to not believe this is a Spanish bar

GRILLED GAMBAS WITH CHORIZO BUTTER, LEMON AND AIOLI

SERVES 4

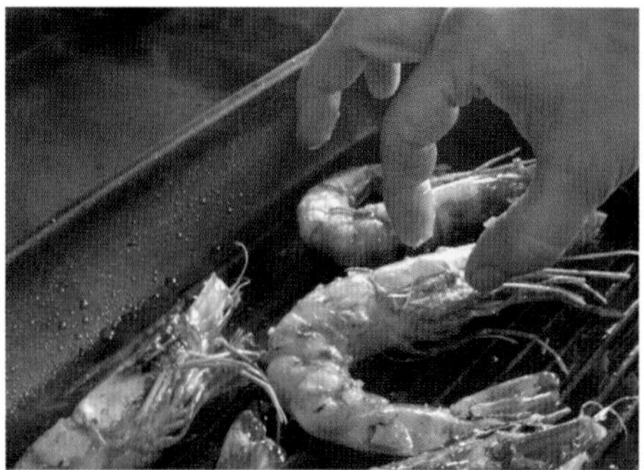

Ingredients

Gambas

12 Gambas
3/4 pint olive oil
zest and juice of 1 lemon
2 garlic cloves, finely diced
1 bunch of thyme
6 wooden skewers
2 lemons for garnishing
paprika for dusting

Chorizo Butter

125g mini Catalan chorizo picante
250g lightly salted butter
25g paprika picante
100ml red wine
50ml Cabernet Sauvignon vinegar
200g Fritarda sauce
balsamic vinegar
parsley oil

Aioli

4 egg yolks
50ml white wine vinegar
25g Dijon mustard
6 cloves garlic, crushed to a paste
juice of 1 lemon
1.3 litres vegetable oil
salt and pepper for seasoning

Method

For the gambas

Peel the Gambas leaving the head and tail on. Put 3 prawns on each skewer, place into a container and cover with the olive oil, zest of 1 lemon, diced garlic and thyme. Leave to marinate for a maximum of 24 hours.

For the chorizo butter

Cut chorizo into rings and place under the grill on a medium heat. Allow for some of the excess fat to come out of the chorizo then remove the pan from under the grill and place onto the stove. Once the pan is hot, deglaze with the red wine and vinegar and cook until reduced by half then blend to form a thick puree. Set aside to cool.

Once cool, add the softened butter, paprika picante, and lemon juice. Mix well. Place the mixture on to a piece of cling film and roll tightly to form a sausage shape. Place in the refrigerator to set.

For the aioli

Mix together egg yolks, white wine vinegar and mustard to a paste. Add crushed garlic, then slowly whisk in the oil until the aioli reaches a smooth consistency. Finally, whisk in the lemon juice and season to taste with salt and pepper. Refrigerate until needed.

To serve

Take the skewered prawns and place on a hot char-grill, or grill pan. Cook for 1 minute on each side. Heat a sauté pan, add 100g of the chorizo butter and cook until foaming and add the grilled prawns for 20 seconds only. Remove from the pan and place on to serving plates.

Dress the plates by firstly dusting with paprika, then add the Fritarda sauce, parsley oil and balsamic and serve with the aioli and fresh lemon wedges.

Pepper puree £7.50
and Morcilla
£9.50
Toasted Pine
Basque Style

SEA BASS WITH CHARLOTTE POTATOES, MUSSELS AND CHORIZO

SERVES 4

Ingredients

4 x 200g fillets of sea bass with skin on (cut in half on an angle across the fillet)
50ml extra virgin olive oil
50g butter
50g rock salt (Halen Môn's spiced salt works best)
200g charlotte potatoes (cut into 1 inch thick slices)
150g mini Catalan chorizo
2tbsp chopped parsley
12 pea shoots

The Dressing

150ml extra virgin olive oil
100ml sherry vinegar
150g cherry tomatoes, halved
100g mussels (unshelled weight)
100g peas

Method

Season the fish fillets with salt and pepper and set aside. Heat the olive oil in a heavy-bottomed non stick frying pan. Place the fillets skin side down and cook for 1-2 minutes until the skin becomes crisp and golden. Add the butter to the pan and baste the fish, turn the fish over and cook for a further minute. Remove the fillets and keep warm but not hot or they will continue to cook.

Using the pan the fish was cooked in, add a little more olive oil then add the Charlotte potatoes and chorizo sausage. Carefully cook together until the oil from the chorizo colours the potatoes, regulate the heat to make sure the chorizo doesn't burn. Finally, add the chopped parsley.

For the dressing

Whisk together the olive oil and sherry vinegar, Gently warm in a saucepan but do not over heat. Add the cherry tomato halves and cook slowly until the tomatoes start to wilt. Add the mussels and warm through. Finally add the peas and again, warm them through taking care not to overcook.

To serve

Place the potato and chorizo mix into the centre of the plate, top with the sea bass fillets serving skin side up. Spoon the warmed dressing and peas around the plate and finish with a drizzle of aged balsamic and the pea shoots.

CHOCOLATE FONDUE WITH MARSHMALLOWS AND FRUIT

SERVES 4

Method

For the chocolate sauce

In a saucepan bring all the ingredients to the boil, add the cream and bring back to the boil then simmer for approx 5 minutes or until the Mars Bar has completely dissolved. Pass through a sieve and set aside.

To serve

Onto a serving plate of your choice, arrange the marshmallows, followed by the strawberries, banana and tangerines. Sprinkle on the raspberries and physallis and dust with icing sugar. Serve alongside the hot chocolate sauce and provide small forks for dipping the fruit into the sauce.

Ingredients

For the chocolate sauce

125g caster sugar
125g water
40g cocoa powder
250g double cream
1 Mars Bar, chopped up

Fruit

12-15 marshmallows
2 bananas cut into 2 inch slices
12 strawberries
2 tangerines peeled and segmented
10 raspberries
6 physallis
icing sugar for decoration

Snacks
Valencia
Spanish
Iberico

088 ESTBEK HOUSE

East Row, Sandsend, Whitby, North Yorkshire YO21 3SU

01947 893 424
www.estbekhouse.co.uk

With an aim of: 'To create somewhere we would like to eat and stay' – Estbek is always developing and moving forward. We strive to ensure guests are offered a uniquely different and caring restaurant, where the natural flavours of our ingredients are allowed to shine through - without the complications of many flavours often seen as 'en-vogue' for restaurants - a firework show of flavour on the plate may be dazzling but so is that lone wild spring flower, this philosophy being very much evident in Estbek's approach to its seafood as well their own vegetable plot and free range chickens – which Tim Lawrence (chef and co-owner) say's their eggs make fantastic brulee's!

This award-winning restaurant with the back drop of Sandsend, one of Yorkshire's hidden gems is now at the forefront of the region's accommodation, with all rooms benefiting from the present owners' refurbishment and most importantly ongoing improvements and attention in both accommodation and restaurant, ensuring that your special evening and stay is as enjoyable and memorable as we can help make it!

Estbek also balances its menu with a unique Antipodean wine list, matching flavours with some of the finest and rarest wines that can be found, also proud to work with many wineries selecting and shipping a selection of wines only available at Estbek.

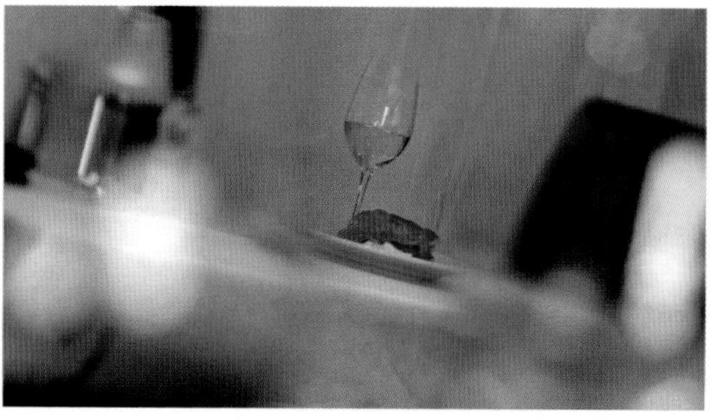

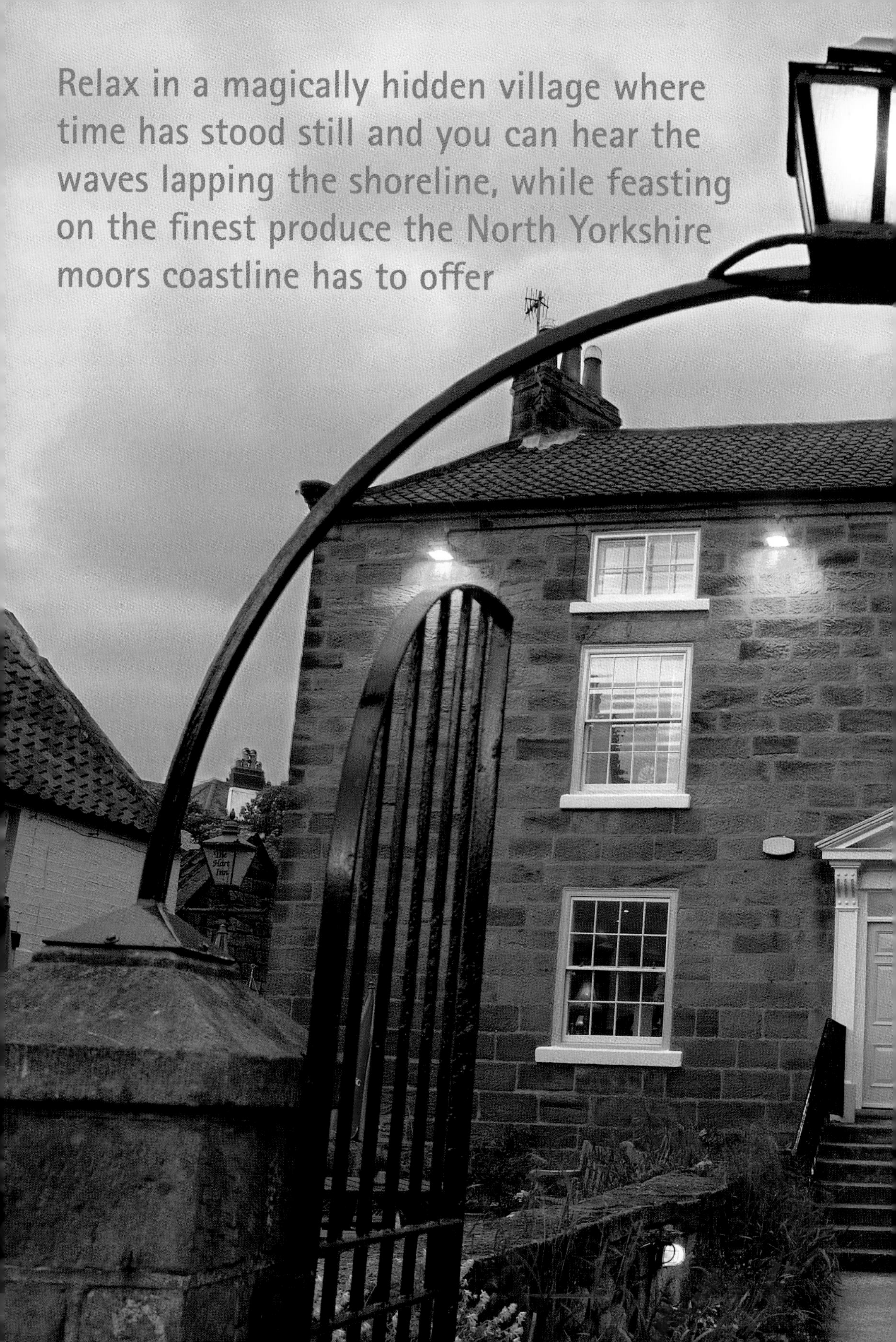
Relax in a magically hidden village where time has stood still and you can hear the waves lapping the shoreline, while feasting on the finest produce the North Yorkshire moors coastline has to offer

Tel. 01947 · 893424
Restaurant
Opening at...
6PM
Today
Accommodation
NO VACANCIES
Entrance
Entrance

WILD MUSHROOM BASKET

SERVES 4

Ingredients

Mushroom Stock

20g onion finely chopped
5ml olive oil
1 clove crushed garlic
100g button mushrooms
200ml water
seasoning
Plus any large stalks from the wild mushrooms (see wild mushroom filling recipe below)

Bubble and Squeak Basket

100g thinly sliced red onion
300g peeled potatoes
100g peeled, diced and par cooked carrots
100g shredded savoy cabbage
1 tbsp Worcestershire sauce
1tbsp of mushroom stock
1 clove of crushed garlic
2 finely chopped spring onions
olive oil for frying
salt and ground white pepper

Mushroom Sauce

mushroom stock from above
300ml double cream

Wild Mushroom Filling

250g mixed wild mushroom (sliced with excess stalks reserved for stock)
20g diced white onion
10ml olive oil
1 clove crushed garlic
5g butter

Method

For the mushroom stock

Into a medium sized pan add the olive oil and then soften the onion, add the mushrooms and garlic and enough water to just cover the mushrooms.

Place on a rolling boil until all the ingredients are softened.

Season well and allow to cool slightly before pouring in to a blender to blend.

For the bubble and squeak basket

Boil and mash the potatoes, place to one side.

Place a large frying pan or wok on a high heat, add oil and butter then add the onion, garlic, cabbage and carrot.

Fry till softened then add the mushroom stock and Worcestershire sauce.

Add the mix to the mashed potato, season well and add the chopped spring onion.

Mix together well and place the bubble and squeak into food rings creating a well in the centre to form a basket shape.

Place on a baking tray bake at 220°C (Gas mark 7) for 20-25 minutes.

For the mushroom sauce

Heat the double cream in a pan and add 3-4 tablespoons of the mushroom stock, then boil until it thickens.

Check for seasoning; keep warm while assembling the dish.

For the wild mushroom filling

(this stage needs doing just before serving)

Heat a fry pan or wok, add the butter and olive oil, then add the onion, garlic and season.

Fry until just starting to soften then put in the sliced mushrooms and fry lightly until softened.

To serve

Place the bubble and squeak baskets onto a greased baking tray, remove food rings and place into a pre-heated oven (220°C), before starting to cook the mushroom filling.

Divide the mushrooms between the baskets and pop back into the oven while you warm the sauce.

Remove the baskets from the baking tray using a spatula and place onto serving plates.

Pour mushroom sauce around the edge of the basket.

Garnish and serve.

ESTBEK'S SEAFOOD PIE

SERVES 1

Ingredients

113g of white fish cut into ounce pieces, (we always use Halibut, Silver Hake, Cod)
85g of prawns or crayfish tails
28g brown shrimp (peeled)
a little lobster and a lobster claw(shelled)
150ml double cream
fresh chopped parsley (to garnish)
fresh lemon juice (half a lemon)
2 fresh king scallop (sliced)
a small haveful of samphire, kale or spinach

Method

Pour the cream into a non-stick pan, add lemon juice, salt pepper, and the herbs.

Reduce down till the cream thickens, then add the fish pieces and turn off the heat

In the mean time place an oven proof dish in a pre heated oven (moderate heat) and start heating a (non-stick) frying pan on the stove top.

Now the sauce has cooled a little add the rest of the seafood.

Drizzle olive oil over the scallops and season with lemon juice, salt and black pepper.

Blanch the Samphire (or spinach / kale) and re-heat the sauce.

Place the Samphire (etc) into the warmed dish, pour the fish and sauce over.

Ensure the pan is hot for the scallops. Place into the pan searing for 20 seconds, on one side only, until the scallop surface facing towards you starts to change from a translucent to opaque.

Place on top of the seafood, sprinkle with chopped parsley.

To serve

Serve with potatoes and vegetables or your choice.

Tim's Tips

The heat from the sauce starts cooking the fish, make sure the fish is not over cooked; it needs to be kept in nice chunks.

When searing the scallops again do not overcook, you need a nice hot smoking pan and in for 20 seconds.

LEMON MERINGUE

SERVES 4

Ingredients

lemon curd (please see below)
meringue (about 2 small nests in size)
200ml whipped cream
(add a quick slash of vanilla essence and a little sprinkle of sugar to the cream before you whip)
4 scoops of good quality vanilla ice-cream
handful of almonds to decorate

Estbek Lemon Curd

(makes 2 – 3 Jars)
2 lemons (juice and rind)
2 free range eggs
55g butter
225g sugar

Method

You can make this dessert into individual pudding dishes or into one large dish which you can serve from.

For the lemon curd

Fill a saucepan with water (approximately half full), and place on a medium heat. Take 3 jars and lids and wash in hot water, rinse and fill with boiling water, allow to stand.

Grate the rind of the lemons and squeeze out the juice.

Put sugar, rind and juice, butter and beaten eggs into a large glass or metal basin (which will sit on top of the saucepan with the base just above the water).

Place bowl on top of a saucepan of simmering water.

Stir with a wooden spoon until thick and the curd coats the back of the spoon.

Empty the hot water out of the jars, allow to drain for a few moments and then pour the curd into the jars and seal.

Once cooled to room temperature, refrigerate, this will keep for up to two weeks.

To serve

Place a spoonful of cream into the base of the dish. Next add a few pieces of broken meringue on top of the cream, followed by one scoop of vanilla ice-cream. Top with a good spoon full of lemon curd.

Decorate with almonds (toasted) – or grated lemon and lime zest. Serve and enjoy!

098
THE FOURTH FLOOR CAFÉ AND BAR AT HARVEY NICHOLS

107-111 Briggate, Leeds LS1 6AZ

0113 204 8000
www.harveynichols.com

Harvey Nichols Fourth Floor café and bar is located in the heart of Leeds City Centre. With views over the city the restaurant's bright and airy space has always been a favourite meeting place for fashion lovers and foodies alike and after 14 years continues to be so.

The versatility of the space ensures that as the day progresses, so does the ambience, making it the perfect meeting place. From new mums catching up, to chief executives doing deals and romantic couples falling in love, the restaurant is a welcoming environment with menus to reflect the eclectic crowd.

Menus include a breakfast and light bar snack menu. For an indulgent treat there is the afternoon tea menu as well as a selection of hand made patisseries and decadent desserts.

For lunch and dinner there is both an a la carte and prix fix menu. Both are designed and edited by Richard Walton Allen the Fourth Floor's executive chef ensuring there is always, seasonal, locally sourced and excellent quality options whether you want a speedy business lunch, a relaxing celebration or to catch up with friends and loved ones.

Serving everything from coffee to signature cocktails, the bar offers a stylish and comfortable setting for a shopping pit stop, a pre dinner cocktail, date night or a girls night out.

Now open five nights a week, the Fourth Floor's menus and extensive wine list, plus regular special menus and events offer a versatile and exclusive dining experience.

The team at Harvey Nichols Leeds, led by executive chef Richard Walton Allen, endeavour to source the best locally sourced produce to create seasonal menus exclusively for the Leeds Fourth Floor Café and Bar

EAST COAST CRAB, TOMATO AND AVOCADO SALSA AND BROWN CRAB DRESSING

SERVES 4

For this dish we use live crabs from the east coast and cook them ourselves. You can of course use high quality cooked crab meat, one good way of buying this is to buy dressed crabs and separate the white and brown meat.

Ingredients

1 whole crab (approximately 2kg)
4 plum tomatoes
1 ripe avocado
2 tbsp crème fraîche
1 tbsp Worcestershire sauce
dash Tabasco
small punnet baby watercress
dash lemon juice
dash olive oil
sourdough roll

Method

Before cooking you first must humanely kill the crab.

Boil the crab in a large pan of water with a generous handful of sea salt.

Immerse fully in the boiling water for 12 minutes.

Take out and drain on its side before plunging into ice cold water to cool, remove from water after 10 minutes, drain well and chill thoroughly.

Remove the front claws and the rear claws.

Crack the front claws with the flat of a heavy knife, carefully pick out the claw meat - disposing of the shell. (Keep this meat in a separate container.)

Now remove the underbelly of the crab in one swift pull, remove and dispose of the grey fingers and any of the membrane around the outer brown meat. (The brown meat is easily removed with a spoon.)

Check over the white meat again for any shell and chill both the brown and white meat until needed.

For the dressing

Take half of the brown meat and put in a high speed blender.

Now add the crème fraîche, Worcestershire sauce and Tabasco along with a little ground pepper. Blend for 1 minute and then sieve through a conical strainer.

Deseed the tomatoes and dice finely, peel and dice the avocado and mix with the tomato. Add a little lemon juice and a drizzle of olive oil to this mixture.

To serve

Carefully spoon two lines of white crab meat onto a long plate, with a line of the salsa in the middle. Add the dressing in a line and garnish with the baby watercress and toasted sourdough bread.

HAREWOOD ESTATE VENISON COOKED TWO WAYS

SERVES 4

We are lucky enough to be able to use the fantastic deer from the nearby Harewood Estate, just outside of Leeds. The deer are fantastic creatures to watch in their own habitat and they are well looked after by the team at Harewood.

Ingredients

200g topside venison
1 small venison shoulder
1 bottle Beaujolais wine
200g butter
100ml cream
2 brown onions
2 carrots
1 celeriac
1litre chicken stock
1 Savoy cabbage
3 potatoes
1 white onion
handful fresh wild mushrooms
small bunch thyme

Method

For the shoulder of venison

To braise the shoulder, trim it of any obvious fat or sinew, cut the shoulder so it lays flat. Season with white pepper and a little salt, leave to one side.

Now peel and chop the brown onions, carrots and half of the celeriac. Chop into medium size chunks around the size of a golf ball. In a large casserole pan (must be oven proof) add a little oil and brown the venison shoulder well on all sides.

Once browned, remove from the pan and then add the vegetables to the pan. Brown these quickly then add half a bottle of Beaujolais.

Reduce the wine until it is a sticky consistency in the bottom of the pan. Quickly put the venison back in and add the chicken stock just so it covers the meat and vegetables. Add the thyme, put on a lid or tight foil and place into an oven that is set to 120°C.

Braise the meat turning twice for 90 minutes. Leave to stand in the juice for 1 hour before draining. Strain the juice back over the meat, discard the vegetables and herbs.

For the potatoes

Peel and cut the potatoes into 3cm high cylinders with a pastry cutter (you should have 4-6). In a small cold pan cut slices of the butter to lie in the bottom, covering the base. Place your potato's cylinders in here upright.

Now season the potatoes and put on a high heat, the butter will melt around them. Once the butter turns brown - quickly and carefully add a small cup of water. Put them in a hot oven covered with greaseproof paper, they will take around 25-30 minutes to cook.

For the cabbage

Slice thinly and blanch in boiling hot water. Refresh in cold water and drain, then put to one side.

For the topside of venison

Pour 6 tablespoons of the venison cooking stock in a shallow pan, reduce slightly then add the shoulder. Warm through, glazing with little more stock if needed. Now heat a frying pan until hot and carefully place in the venison topside and add a knob of butter. Turn twice so all sides are sealed, baste with the butter, keep the pan on the heat but turn down. Now in a small pan warm the cabbage in a knob of butter, season well and add the cream. Sauté the wild mushrooms in a frying pan and season.

To serve

Place a small spoon of cabbage on each plate along with a small chunk of the shoulder, carve the topside in pieces and arrange along the cabbage.

Scatter the wild mushrooms around the dish and add one potato per portion, spoon a little sauce over.

TRIO OF BLACKBERRY DESSERTS

SERVES 4

Blackberries, or "Brambles" to give them their Yorkshire name, are our favourite soft fruit, so versatile with a great balance of sweet and acidic flavours. We get ours from Makins Farm, approximately 6 miles outside Leeds and it has its own airstrip!

This dish has three components, all can be made in advance and served by themselves at any time!

Ingredients

Port and Blackberry Jelly

450g blackberries
225g caster sugar
30ml crème de mure
150ml port
300ml water
4 leafs gelatine

Blackberry Sorbet

Makes a 2 litre ice cream size tub
2kg blackberry purée
1.5kg caster sugar
1.5 litre water
peel of 1 lemon

Blackberry Frangipane

250g fresh blackberries
375g good quality unsalted butter
375g caster sugar
375g ground almonds
28g plain flour
4 medium free range eggs

Method

For the port and blackberry jelly

Place the blackberries, 150ml water and sugar in a saucepan, slowly bring to the boil (if done too quickly the flavour will be affected.)

Simmer on a very low heat for 5 minutes.

Take off the heat and strain through a fine strainer, discard the pulp.

Soak the 4 gelatine leaves in 150ml of water until soft. Remove from water and whisk into the hot blackberry mixture.

Now add the port and crème de mure.

Set in shallow dishes or glasses around 100ml size and garnish with one blackberry.

For the blackberry sorbet

Dissolve the sugar and water in a pan and add the lemon peel. Warm slowly until all sugar is dissolved. Strain the mixture and chill.

Once cold add the blackberry purée then mix thoroughly.

Churn in an ice cream maker - following the instructions from the manufacturer.

Once churned, freeze until needed. Keep in a sealed container

For the blackberry frangipane

Cream soft butter and sugar together in a mixing bowl.

Break eggs into a small bowl and beat.

Gradually add the egg into the butter and sugar mix, continue stirring.

Now sieve in the flour, add the almonds and stir in gently using a large spoon.

The mixture will look a little split - don't worry!

Place mixture in small tart cases or a flexible mini bun case adding one or two blackberries per tart.

Bake at 160°C for around 10 minutes until golden brown.

To serve

Place the blackberry jelly on a large oval plate in the middle with a warm frangipane at the side.

Add a scoop of sorbet with a small biscuit underneath to stop any sliding of the desserts. Garnish with a small spoon of clotted cream and mint.

108 THE HEPWORTH

Sheffield Road, Near Hepworth, Holmfirth HD9 7TP

01484 683 775
www.thehepworth.co.uk

The Hepworth Restaurant stands high on the hill having been recently transformed in November 2010 into a country chic retreat from three 300 year old cottages. Nestled in the beautiful, picturesque and scenic Pennine countryside of Holme Valley, Yorkshire born owners Jonathan Tiffany and Kristieanne Travers have turned the restaurant into an escape from the bustling world to envelope a scene of understated luxury, encasing original beams, exposed stone walls and wooden lintel windows together with grand ornate mirrors, granite bar tops and dining tables dressed with crisp white linen and candles to create an inviting and subtle elegance.

The menu at The Hepworth extends from contemporary Classic British dishes to more diverse flavours and influences from other countries with an artful modern twist. 'Yorkshire Life reader award winner' Head Chef Richard Whittaker along with his dedicated and passionate kitchen team ensure seasonal interest, originality, flair and pride themselves in a commitment to using only the freshest of locally sourced ingredients available.

The wine list has been meticulously chosen to complement each dish served, showcasing around 60 different bottles of Wines and Champagnes from around the world whilst being served by very knowledgeable and conscientious staff. In the warmer months diners can sit outside and enjoy a light lunch, sandwich or cocktails whilst enjoying the exceptional views.

The new entrance and bar area at The Hepworth sets the scene for a relaxing and indulgent experience to come, sit at high champagne wooden poseur tables, listen to music being played from the Baby Grand Piano or simply indulge and enjoy a bottle of Dom Perignon in the private Champagne booth area

RABBIT AND PLUM TART, YORKSHIRE BLUE AND MUSTARD SAUCE, HOT APPLE JELLY

SERVES 4

Ingredients

Rabbit Tart

½ tsp wine vinegar
¼ tsp salt
500g diced rabbit
50g plain flour
1 rasher chopped smoked bacon
½ finely diced onion
½ diced apple
3 plums, stoned and chopped
15g brown sugar
160ml bitter

Hot Water Pastry

225g plain flour
25ml milk
25ml water
75g lard
½ egg yolk beaten

Yorkshire Blue and Mustard Sauce

½ finely diced banana shallot
½ clove finely chopped garlic
50ml rabbit stock (made from bones)
½ tsp wholegrain mustard
25g grated Yorkshire blue cheese
15ml calvados

Hot Apple Jelly

400ml quality apple juice
1 ½ tsp lemon juice
50g caster sugar
1 ½ tsp agar (vegetarian gelatine)

Method

For the rabbit tart

Marinade rabbit in water, salt and vinegar overnight.

Drain and flour meat, add oil to hot pan and brown meat, add onions, bacon, apple, plums and sugar.

Cook until onions are soft and brown. Add beer and simmer for 2 hours.

For the hot water pastry

Boil milk, water and lard in a pan. Add egg to flour in a separate bowl, pour over liquid. Knead until dough.

Roll out thinly, cut into a disc with a mousse ring and then cut a long strip that measures the circumference of the ring. Place inside ring to make pastry cup.

Cook in preheated oven (200°C) for 20 minutes.

Leave pastry to cool and add warm rabbit filling.

For the yorkshire blue and mustard sauce

Sweat shallots in oil, add garlic, mustard and brandy. Reduce to syrup. Add stock, reduce by half and add cheese and season.

For the hot apple jelly

Heat juices and sugar to boiling point then whisk in Agar.

Set in mould lined with cling film and place in fridge till set. Cut and warm jelly gently in oven to serve.

Jelly will melt if it reaches above 80°C.

To serve

As seen in picture.

THE HEPWO

ROASTED BREAST OF PHEASANT, ROLLED THIGH STUFFED WITH BLACK PUDDING, LOLLIPOP LEG, SOURED WHITE CABBAGE, ALE JUS

SERVES 4

Ingredients

Soured Cabbage

50g goose fat
½ finely sliced large onion
1 rasher chopped smoked bacon
3 cloves finely chopped garlic
½ white cabbage finely sliced
5 crushed juniper berries
2 bay leaves
75ml cider vinegar
25g sugar
35cl Riesling wine

Pheasant

2 whole pheasant
50g black pudding

Ale Jus

¼ finely diced onion
¼ clove finely chopped garlic
½ pint ale
½ pint pheasant stock (made from carcass)
½ tbsp redcurrant jelly

Method

For the soured cabbage

Melt goose fat in large pan, add onions and sweat until translucent.

Add bacon, garlic and cabbage, sweat for 5 minutes. Add juniper berries, bay leaves, vinegar and sugar.

Cook until a syrup consistency forms. Pour in white wine and reduce until liquid reduces. Take out bay leaves and season.

For the pheasant

Take legs off the bird, cut breast from carcass. Separate the thigh and the leg at the joint.

Bone the thigh and fill the centre with the black pudding, roll and tie with string.

Cut the skin at top of leg and pull the skin off, cut meat downwards and pull down, place a cloth on the tendons and pull to remove each one. Push meat down until you have a ball.

Place breast, lollipop leg and stuffed thigh in a hot pan with olive oil and seal. Season.

Place in a preheated oven (190°C). After 6 minutes take out breast and rest. After another 5 minutes take out thigh and leg. Slice breast and thigh to serve.

For the ale jus

Sweat onions in heavy bottomed pan until translucent, add garlic and sweat for a further 2 minutes.

Add ale and reduce by a half, add stock and reduce by a half again.

Add redcurrant jelly and simmer for 5 minutes.

To serve

As seen in picture.

BERRY MERINGUE CHEESECAKE, GIN AND TONIC SORBET

SERVES 6

Ingredients

Cheesecake

500g cream cheese
2 beaten eggs
75g caster sugar
½ vanilla pod (seeds only)
juice of ¼ lemon
200g mixed berries
200ml water
pinch salt
8 digestive biscuits
85g unsalted butter melted

Gin and Tonic Sorbet

200ml cold water
150g caster sugar
150ml tonic water
25ml Bombay Sapphire gin
juice of 1 lemon
½ tsp liquid glucose

Italian Meringue

30ml water
15g liquid glucose
150g caster sugar
3 egg whites

Method

For the cheesecake

Mix digestive biscuits and melted butter in a blender.

Heat berries in a pan with water until reduced. Cool.

In a separate bowl put cream cheese and add lemon, sugar, vanilla and salt. Mix well, add eggs and cooled berry mixture, and mix again.

Grease mousse rings and place on a tray lined with parchment paper. Spoon heaped tablespoon of the biscuit in to the moulds and press down with the end of a rolling pin to create the base.

Add cheesecake mix on top to nearly full.

Place in a preheated oven (175°C) for 12 minutes until firm with a slight wobble in middle. Cool.

For the gin and tonic sorbet

Boil sugar and water in a pan and take off heat, add glucose and tonic and chill in fridge. When cooled add gin and lemon juice, churn in an ice cream machine until set.

For the italian meringue

Boil sugar, glucose and water till 110°C. Start whisking egg whites in a mixer until stiff. When sugar is 115°C, very slowly add to the whites while still whisking, keep whisking until cooled (approximately 15 minutes).

Place in piping bag with a star nozzle.

To serve

Push cheesecake out of ring and place on plate. Pipe the meringue in a circular motion on top of the cheesecake.

Brown meringue with a kitchen blowtorch (optional).

Serve cheesecake with a scoop of sorbet, a berry coulis and fresh berries.

HEPWORTH

118
HOTEL DU VIN & BISTRO

88 The Mount, York YO24 1AX

01904 557 350
www.hotelduvin.com

Located in the tranquil area known as The Mount, close to the city's historic centre, Hotel du Vin York is a beautiful Grade II-listed building that dates back to the early 19th century.

Formerly a private home and an orphanage, the hotel houses 44 stylish bedrooms and suites, a beautiful bar, two private dining rooms and of course its Trademark Bistro. A relaxing haven serving stunning culinary classics.

Ricky Murray head chef at the Bistro du Vin is well qualified to run the award winning Kitchen, having started his career at the Four Seasons Hotel in Dublin at the tender age of 19. He joined the Malmaison & Hotel du Vin Group in 2005 at the Malmaison Birmingham then transferred to Malmaison Leeds to take the position of Sous Chef; then in 2010 took his first Head Chef position at the Hotel du Vin York. Ricky prides himself on sourcing local ingredients and supporting Yorkshire suppliers, and he champions our Home Grown and Local philosophy daily through his menu.

The Bistro boasts an extensive wine list of over 500 bins; you are guaranteed to be advised on the perfect wine selection for your meal courtesy of our dedicated in house Sommelier team.

The Hotel du Vin prides itself on being able to cater for any of your requirements; menus can be created upon request for wedding parties and private dining. We also have an exciting and very popular event calendar including Wine Dinners that run throughout the Year.

Hotel du Vin
&
Bistro

The Bistro boasts an extensive wine list of over 500 bins; you are guaranteed to be advised on the perfect wine selection for your meal courtesy of our dedicated in house Sommelier team

PAN SEARED KING SCALLOPS, CARAMELISED CAULIFLOWER PURÉE, BLACK PUDDING

SERVES 4

Method

Place a medium sized saucepan on to heat.

Take the cauliflower remove outer leaves and quarter, remove core and roughly chop.

Add 100g butter to the pan with cauliflower and fry till golden brown and soft.

Place in a food processor and blitz to a smooth paste, reserve to one side and cut black pudding into a small triangle.

Take scallops and remove orange roe and sinew then season.

Heat a frying pan till almost smoking, add oil, place seasoned scallops into the pan and cook for roughly 30 seconds to a minute and turn and repeat. Now add the black pudding (depending on the size of the scallop and how you like them cooked the time will vary), you're looking for the scallop to turn a golden brown colour.

Heat through the cauliflower purée.

To serve

Serve immediately, garnishing with the Red Amaranth (optional).

Ingredients

12 large king scallops
1 small cauliflower
80g Doreen's black pudding
100g butter
5g Red Amaranth micro herb (optional)

PAN ROASTED DUCK BREAST, PEPPERED SWEDE, CHESTNUT CRUSTED PARSNIPS, MULLED WINE JUS

SERVES 4

Ingredients

4 duck breasts

Peppered Swede

1 large swede (peeled and diced into cm chunks)
1tsp black pepper
5g sea salt
100g butter

Chestnut Crusted Parsnips

2 large parsnips (peeled and cut into batons with core removed)
1 egg beaten
100g chestnuts
50g bread crumbs
20g plain flour
50g butter

Mulled Wine Jus

100ml reduced beef stock
100ml red wine
25ml dark rum
25ml brandy
3cm cinnamon stick
1 nutmeg crushed
1/4 orange zest
1 tsp orange flower honey
1 tbsp raisins

Method

For the peppered swede

Place diced swede and black pepper into a saucepan, cover with cold water and bring to the boil. Reduce to a simmer and cook till tender (about 10 minutes).

Strain and crush swede with butter, reserve to one side.

For the chestnut crushed parsnips

Take the parsnip batons and boil in well seasoned water till al dente then strain and cool.

Chop up chestnuts until nice and fine, mix with the bread crumbs and sea salt.

Dry parsnips with a clean tea towel, coat with the flour, and shake off any excess.

Dip into the beaten egg.

Now coat with chestnut mix and return egg mix to double coat with chestnuts.

Heat frying pan, add butter and fry parsnips till golden brown.

Season.

For the mulled wine jus

Take all ingredients except the stock and place in a small saucepan, reduce in volume by half.

Add the stock and reduce by a quarter.

Place to one side to infuse then strain.

For the duck

Pre heat oven to 180°C.

Season each duck breast and rub with a little oil.

Heat a large frying pan to smoking point, add a little oil and place the duck breast skin side down till crisp and golden, turn and seal the flesh.

Place in the oven at 180°C for 5 minutes, remove and rest for 4 minutes in a warm place. Meanwhile reheat the swede, jus and parsnips for serving.

To serve

Quickly flash duck in the oven for 1 minute and arrange as seen in the picture.

SPICED CARROT CAKE, COINTREAU AND MANDARIN SORBET

SERVES 4

Ingredients

Spiced Carrot Cake

1 egg
100g caster sugar
86g vegetable oil
1/4 fresh vanilla pod
115g plain flour
1 pinch of salt
1/4 tsp Bicarbonate of soda
1/4 tsp ground cinnamon
1/4 tsp ground ginger
1/4 whole nutmeg grated
275g grated carrot
25g crushed walnuts
50g sultanas

Cointreau and Mandarin Sorbet

240ml caster sugar
475ml water
310g mandarin orange segments
60ml lemon juice,
20ml Cointreau

Stock syrup recipe

2 oranges (juiced and zested)
2 lemons (juiced and zested)
1/4 cinnamon stick
1/4 vanilla pod
500g sugar
1 litre water
1 cardamom pod
1/2 star anise

Carrot Purée

250g carrots
500ml stock syrup

Method

For the spiced carrot cake

Place egg and sugar in a mixing bowl and beat till light and fluffy.

Add vegetable oil slowly.

Add remaining ingredients except flour and mix well.

Sieve flour and fold through mix.

Line a cake tin with grease proof paper.

Add cake mix and bake at 175°C for 35 minutes.

Allow to cool slightly and remove from tin. Don't portion until cool.

For the cointreau and mandarin sorbet

Combine caster sugar and water. Heat them over a low heat until sugar has dissolved, bringing them to boiling point before cooling.

Blend the mandarins to a purée.

Add purée with juice and liqueur to the sugar syrup, combine well.

Pour into bowl and freeze until firm. Stir occasionally.

For the stock syrup recipe

Add all ingredients together in a pan bring to the boil and remove from heat.

Allow to infuse for 30 minutes and strain through a fine sieve.

For the carrot purée

Place peeled and diced carrot into a pan, add stock syrup and cook until tender.

Add to a food processor, blitz till mixture is smooth, then cool.

To serve

Portion cake and serve with the carrot purée and Cointreau and mandarin sorbet.

128 THE OLD VICARAGE

Ridgeway Moor, Ridgeway Village, Near Sheffield S12 3XW

01142 475 814
www.theoldvicarage.co.uk

The Old Vicarage is a delightful old Country House offering a comfortable and homely atmosphere, with gastronomy and service of the highest standard.
Set in acres of gardens, the house commands stunning views over open countryside; its gently-rolling lawns and copses blending with the surrounding countryside of the Moss Valley conservation area. Inside the house you will be cosseted in a calming ambience of fine fabrics, Persian carpets, original paintings and, in the winter time, a blazing log fire.....
Whether you visit for business entertaining or private dining, the focus of the experience at The Old Vicarage is the remarkable and innovative Michelin Starred cooking. The Old Vicarage menu is grounded in nature and evocative of the seasons – Tessa's work revolves around the Vicarage kitchen garden and the produce from the local farms and smallholders in the neighbouring villages. For the past 24 years we have been using organic, locally grown produce, wild and foraged woodland ingredients, and traditionally butchered meats from prize winning rare-breed herds – a long time before these labels became trendy buzzwords!
The owners are also wine merchants and importers so, as might be expected, the wine selection is exceptional. There is a multiple award-winning wine list, representing the best quality and value across a wide price range, from the modest to the iconic.

As well as classics from top estates in Burgundy, Bordeaux, Rhône, Spain and Italy, the list also features some of the best examples of progressive winemaking from boutique wineries in The Americas and the Southern Hemisphere.
A visit to The Old Vicarage is an unforgettable experience!

Set in acres of gardens, the house commands stunning views over open countryside; its gently-rolling lawns and copses blending with the surrounding countryside of the Moss Valley conservation area

ROAST FILLET OF WHITBY COD WITH YORKSHIRE LIQUORICE SAUCE CARAMELISED COB NUTS AND PARSNIP CRISPS

SERVES 6

I find it best to prepare all the garnish bits and the sauce first before cooking the fish.
Pre-heat an oven to 200°C, gas mark 6.

Ingredients

6 x 200g pieces of thick cod fillets (skinned and boned)
2 tbsp olive oil
freshly milled sea salt and black pepper
handful fresh chives, finely chopped

Stock

a few bones to make the stock
½ small onion – peeled and roughly chopped
¼ leek – peeled and roughly chopped
1 stick celery – chopped
1 bay leaf
1 piece lemon zest
5 or 6 black peppercorns
piece star anise

Sauce

small knob of butter
½ small onion finely chopped
2 cloves garlic – peeled and crushed
100g soft liquorice – chopped
150ml fish stock
250ml double cream
½ lime

Caramelised Cob Nuts and Parsnip Crisps

18 cobnuts shelled
4 tbsp caster sugar
1tbps water
2 large parsnips

Method

For the stock

Throw everything for the stock into a pan, cover with water, bring to the boil and simmer for 30 minutes. Strain and keep the clear liquor for sauce. Discard the rest. Reduce the liquor down by half to concentrate the flavour.

For the sauce

Melt the butter in a pan and fry the onion and garlic without colouring. Add the liquorice. Add the stock and then the cream. Keep bubbling on the heat until it has reduced by half. Liquidise and pass through a fine sieve to remove any bits. Season to taste. Add a squeeze of lime to sharpen it.

For the caramelised cob nuts and parsnip crisps

Dissolve the sugar in the water and over a brisk heat cook to a golden caramel. Add the nuts. Pour on to a sheet of parchment paper to cool. When cold enough to handle, break off the caramelised nuts.

Peel the parsnips and slice very thinly using a mandolin. Deep fry half the amount in hot oil until crisp and golden. Drain well and dust lightly with salt. Stir fry the other half in a knob of butter until soft. Sprinkle with a few of the chives.

For the cod

Season the fillets of cod on the underside.

Heat a heavy cast or non-stick pan until evenly very hot. Add a splash of the olive oil.

Put in the cod, top side down and cook, without attempting to move it for 2 or 3 minutes, until golden. The heat of the pan will ensure that it will not stick. Put the pieces into a roasting tin, golden side up and bake in a hot oven for a further 3 or 4 minutes (dependant on the thickness of the fillets) until moist and just cooked. The fish will exude a creamy residue.

To serve

Serve on the buttered parsnip with the nuts on top, the sauce around and a garnish of parsnip crisps.

ROAST RIDGEWAY PARTRIDGE WRAPPED IN PROSCUITTO, SAUTÉED PORCINI AND BLACK PUDDING, CRAB APPLE AND THYME JELLY

SERVES 6

Heat an oven to 200°C, gas mark 6.

Ingredients

6 partridge
6 slices proscuitto
1 chicken breast (skinned)
a good pinch of salt
1 egg white
125ml double cream
olive oil and butter to cook
2 tbsp red wine
10g unsalted butter

2 baking potatoes - peeled
oil for deep fat frying

500g porcini or other wild mushrooms
15g butter
a splash of Madeira
salt & freshly ground black pepper
6 slices of black pudding

Method

Remove the breasts and legs from the birds. Pot-roast the legs in stock with some finely chopped root vegetables and thyme until tender. Chop the chicken breast and process it with the salt and egg white until smooth. Turn into a bowl and using a spatula, gradually work the cream into the mixture until it is absorbed and forms a smooth mousse. Season.

Lay the slices of proscuitto on the work surface, short end nearest to you, and put one breast on the end. Spoon a little mousse onto the breast. Top with the other breast. Roll up away from you in the proscuitto to form a neat roll. Repeat with the other 5 birds.

Sear the breasts with a little oil and butter in a hot pan to seal and colour them. Remove the legs from the cooking liquor and sear in the same pan to colour them.

Roast the partridge legs and breasts for about 10 minutes until cooked and golden. The breasts will be slightly pink inside. Remove and rest in a warm place. Pour 2 tbsp red wine into the roasting pan and reduce over a high heat, scraping up all the roasting juices into it. Press the pot-roasted vegetables and stock through a sieve into the roasting pan and whisk together. Discard the residue. Whisk in the chilled butter to thicken the sauce and give it a gloss. Taste and season.

For the potato crisps

Slice the potatoes thinly on a mandolin. Stack the slices and slice thinly using a sharp knife to make matchstick pieces. Dry them on a tea towel to remove any moisture. Deep-fat fry until golden and crisp. Drain well, and lightly salt.

Wash and dry the porcini and slice into smaller pieces.

Sautée the mushrooms in the butter until softened. Add the Madeira and reduce. Season and add some chopped chives.

Fry the black pudding and plate with a little stir-fried baby spinach. Surround with the mushrooms and top with the partridge and potato.

To serve

Garnish with vegetables and drizzle the sauce around. Serve with crab apple and thyme jelly.

CHOCOLATE AND COGNAC TART WITH MOCHA MOUSSE, ORANGE JELLY AND CHOCOLATE CRISP

SERVES 6

Ingredients

Chocolate, Cognac Tart

Line a 20cm flan tin with rich shortcrust pastry and bake blind. (I use butter shortbread for a richer taste)

180g dark bitter chocolate
5 tbsp Cognac
4 eggs
3 tbsp cornflour
400g caster sugar
600ml single cream
1 vanilla pod
125g unsalted butter softened

Chocolate Crisp

300g dark chocolate
330g egg white plus a pinch of salt
100g sugar
5 egg yolks - beaten

Jelly

180ml dessert wine
90ml Mandarin liqueur
2 leaves gelatine, (soaked in water and squeezed dry)

Mocha Mousse

600ml double cream
450g dark bitter chocolate
1 cup strong espresso - cooled

Sauce

250g extra bitter dark chocolate
250ml double (48%) cream
250g icing sugar - sifted

Method

For the chocolate, cognac tart

Melt chocolate. Beat eggs in bowl. Add cornflour, sugar and 2 tbsp cream and blend well. Bring remaining cream to the boil with the vanilla pod then stir into egg mixture. Remove vanilla pod, add chocolate. Pour into a clean pan and cook gently for 6 or 8 minutes until thickened and the cornflour is cooked. Beat in the butter (the mixture will be very glossy) and pour into the cooked pastry case. Leave to set.

For the chocolate crisp

Melt chocolate. Whisk whites and salt until foamy. Add sugar and whisk until stiff. Add yolks to chocolate and fold in 1/3 whites. When smooth add the rest of meringue. Spread on a non-stick baking tray and bake at 50°C for 6 hours. Cut into shapes at once and leave to cool and crisp.

For the jelly

Warm wine and liqueur. Add gelatine and stir to dissolve. Pour into shallow tray to set. When set cut into cubes

For the mocha mousse

Grate the 450g of chocolate on a coarse grater and melt over a gentle heat in a double boiler until the chocolate is almost melted – it will finish off in its own heat. Remove from the heat, stir in the coffee and allow to cool slightly. Whisk cream to a soft flop. Carefully fold the chocolate into the cream until it is fully combined and smooth. Spoon while still soft.

For the sauce

Melt chocolate and cream together in a double boiler. Gradually beat in the icing sugar until glossy.

To serve

Assemble as in the picture.

138 THE PIPE AND GLASS INN

West End, South Dalton, Beverley, East Yorkshire HU17 7PN

01430 810 246
www.pipeandglass.co.uk

Dating back to the 15th century, the Pipe and Glass Inn stands on the site of the original gatehouse to Dalton Park, still the residence of Lord Hotham. The old gatehouse was eventually replaced by the present building, part of which is 17th century. James and Kate Mackenzie took over The Pipe and Glass Inn in March 2006, and undertook a full refurbishment. The bar has kept a country pub feel, while the restaurant is a warm, welcoming, more contemporary area, with bespoke wooden tables made to James and Kate's specifications, and a conservatory area looking out over the garden and housing a spectacular long table seating up to 24. There is also plenty of room for dining outside.

In 2010 two boutique luxury suites were opened, both with king size beds and their own patios and stunning views into Dalton Park.

Chef-proprietor James is committed to sourcing as much local and seasonal produce as possible – but first and foremost, it's quality that counts. Since opening in 2006 James and Kate have had a philosophy of serving great food with great Yorkshire hospitality.

The Pipe and Glass Inn has gained critical acclaim both locally and nationally, James was recently named 'Yorkshire Life' chef of the year and 'Delicouslyyorkshire' champion. In 2010 The Pipe and Glass was awarded East Yorkshire's first and only Michelin star.

THE
INN

The aim of proprietors James and Kate Mackenzie at the Pipe and Glass Inn is to make our guests feel welcome and comfortable. A Michelin starred country pub serving imaginative local produce and a wide selection of locally brewed real ales

Pipe and Glass Images throughout by Tony Bartholomew

CUBAN MINIS

THE PIPE AND GLASS INN'S SPICED POTTED GLOUCESTER OLD SPOT PORK WITH STICKY APPLE AND CRACKLING SALAD

SERVES 6

Ingredients

Potted Pork

350g cooked pork (hock, shoulder or belly, must have good fat content)
4 tbsp goose fat
2 large shallots finely chopped
12 leaves of sage
2 tbsp capers
8 cornichon
1 tsp mixed spice
salt and black pepper

Sticky Apple

1 granny smith apple
1 litre apple juice
2 tbsp sugar

Garnish

extra goose fat for top of pots
crackling
micro watercress (optional)

Method

Place the chopped cooked pork into a food processor with the goose fat, shallots, capers, cornichon, sage and seasonings. Pulse until a course pâté consistency. If it is a little dry add a little more goose fat. Place potted mixture into pots leaving ½ cm at the top. Spoon on enough melted goose fat to cover all the meat. Place in the fridge for at least 1 hour.

For the sticky apple

Reduce the apple juice and sugar to a caramel, chop the apple then add to the mixture and boil for 2 minutes.

To serve

Place the potted pork on a plate with, watercress, crispy crackling pieces and a spoon of the sticky apple. Alternatively serve the potted mix in a large pot with some good chutney and fresh bread.

GRILLED BARNSLEY CHOP WITH DEVILLED KIDNEYS, NETTLE AND MINT SAUCE

SERVES 4

Ingredients

4 Barnsley lamb chops
a little chopped thyme
4 lamb kidneys
200ml whipping cream
2 tbsp strong English mustard
4 tbsp white breadcrumbs
dash of brandy
1 tsp cayenne pepper
1 tsp chopped parsley
50g butter

4 tbsp nettles (picked / blanched / and roughly chopped)
4 tbsp mint – roughly chopped
4 tbsp white wine vinegar
4 tbsp olive oil

Method

Season the lamb chops with salt, pepper and a little chopped thyme and place on a greased tray under a hot grill for about 10 minutes. Turn after 5 minutes and rest in a warm place.

For the devilled kidneys slice the kidneys in half and cut out the fatty sinew. Heat a little oil in a frying pan and fry the kidneys for about 2 minutes until golden brown and just cooked. Take the kidneys out of the pan and on to an oven proof dish. Deglaze the pan with a little brandy, add cream and mustard and reduce to sauce consistency and pour over the kidneys. Mix the crumbs, butter, parsley and cayenne together in a bowl and then sprinkle over the kidneys and grill until crumbs are golden brown.

To make the sauce place the nettles, mint, white wine vinegar and olive oil in to a liquidiser and purée, check the seasoning.

To serve

Place the chop on your plate with two half kidneys and spoon nettle sauce around. Serve with pickled red cabbage and boulangére potatoes.

TRIO OF YORKSHIRE APPLES APPLE AND BRAMBLE CRUMBLE, STICKY APPLE SPONGE, APPLE SORBET

SERVES 4

Ingredients

Apple Crumble Filling

1kg cooking apples
100g fresh brambles
caster sugar
cinnamon stick

Crumble Topping

200g plain flour
75g demerara sugar
100g butter
50g oats

Sticky Apple

1 litre apple juice
100g sugar
4 eating apples (cut into small dice with skin on)

Sponge

125g butter
125g caster sugar
125g self raising flour
2 eggs
pinch of ground cinnamon
50ml calvados (optional)

Sorbet

4 eating apples (peeled and chopped)
150ml sugar syrup
150ml apple juice
juice of half a lemon

Method

For the crumble topping

Mix the flour and butter to a fine crumb then add the sugar and oats.

For the apple crumble filling

Peel and rough chop the apples, simmer in a pan with the cinnamon, a little water and a lid on until just cooked, remove from heat, add brambles and sugar to taste.

Place the stewed apple mix in 4 little pots and top with the crumble, finish in the oven for 5-10 minutes.

For the sticky apple

Reduce the apple juice and sugar to a thick syrup then add the apple, boil until syrup consistency again.

For the sponge

Beat the butter and sugar, beat in the eggs then fold in flour and cinnamon (and calvados if using).

Steam in individual buttered mould

For the sorbet

Purée the raw apple, place in ice cream machine with all liquid and churn.

To serve

Turn out the sponge onto a presentation plate and spoon over with the sticky apple. Place the hot crumble in the pot and onto the plate. To finish add a ball of sorbet and garnish with fresh brambles and frothy custard.

148 SAMUEL'S AT SWINTON PARK

Swinton Park, Masham, Ripon, North Yorks HG4 4JH

01765 680 900
www.swintonpark.com

For something truly inspiring, the dining room at Swinton Park with its ornate gold leaf ceiling and sweeping views really will take your breath away. This wing of the castellated castle was built in 1890 by the current owner's great-great-great grandfather, and helps create a truly memorable dining experience. The food itself, though, is also cause for celebration.

Guided by the experienced hand of Head Chef, Simon Crannage, the freshness and quality of the ingredients speak for themselves, the style of cuisine being Modern British with a strong seasonal bias.

The commitment to "gate to plate" and low food miles is taken seriously here, and most of the ingredients will have been sourced from the hotel's own four acre walled garden, or from the surrounding 20,000 acre estate (also in the ownership of the Cunliffe-Lister family).

The castle is the stately home of the Earl of Swinton and oozes tradition and grandeur, whilst at the same time offering every contemporary comfort you would expect of a first class hotel. Service is discreet and attentive, and the lavishly furnished drawing room and sitting room, with blazing fires in winter and a terrace and croquet lawn in the summer, entice every guest to linger over an afternoon tea or after dinner coffee. Each of the 30 bedrooms is individually designed, with an exclusive use spa and five treatment rooms for those in need of a little pampering. There is also a wide range of country pursuits on offer, including falconry, golf and fishing, and a cookery school running residential, day and evening courses throughout the year.

Recent accolades for Samuel's include listings in Hardens Guide and AA 3 Rosettes, Hotel of the Year (White Rose Awards 2009) and Good Hotel Guide Family Hotel of the Year 2011.

For those wanting an alternative type of dining experience, the hotel offers demonstration Chef's Table dinners and Sunday Masterclass Lunches, with Wine Dinners planned for 2011 and Deerhouse Barbecues served under the stars in the summer months

TUNA TARTARE, RED PEPPER, BLACK OLIVE, SAFFRON SHALLOTS, CORIANDER, SOUR DOUGH CROUTES

SERVES 4

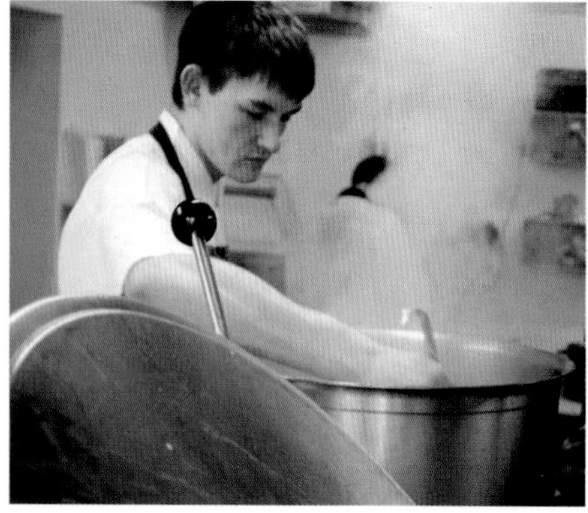

Ingredients

red pepper coulis (see recipe below)
20 cubes of uncooked tuna (1cm dice)
4 sliced cornichons
12 sourdough croutons
black olive powder
4 pink grapefruit segments
micro coriander
saffron shallots (see recipe below)

Red Pepper Coulis

6 red peppers
200ml extra virgin olive oil
juice of ½ lemon
salt and white pepper

Saffron Shallots

3 banana shallots peeled and sliced into rings
350g white wine vinegar
350g water
350g sugar
pinch of saffron

Method

For the pepper coulis

Cut the peppers in half lengthways, put onto a baking tray and drizzle with a little olive oil and salt, roast in the oven at 170°C for 30 minutes or until the skin has blackened. Once cool enough to handle peel the blackened skin from the pepper. Add the flesh to a food processor and blend until smooth, on a low speed add the oil gradually until all of the oil is incorporated. Push though a fine sieve and season with salt, pepper and lemon juice, chill until needed.

For the saffron shallots

In a saucepan add the vinegar, water, sugar and saffron. Bring to the boil. Add the shallots and boil for 1 minute. Remove from the heat and allow to cool. Chill and use as required.

To serve

In a flat serving bowl pour in the red pepper coulis and with the back of a spoon spread out the coulis until the base of the bowl has a shallow covering. Use this as the foundation and then randomly place the rest of the dish items - the tuna, cornichons, croutons, grapefruit segments and the saffron shallots. This is a very trendy and modern way to present food, which is simple to achieve. Finish with the micro coriander and a sprinkling of black olive powder.

ROAST ESTATE PIGEON, RAVIOLI OF WOODLAND MUSHROOMS, WARM CELERIAC COLESLAW

SERVES 4

Ingredients

2 oven ready pigeons
1 block butter (unsalted) for cooking

Ravioli of Woodland Mushroom Pasta

500g pasta flour
8 egg yolks
2 whole eggs
3 tbsp olive oil
3 tbsp water
pinch of salt

Ravioli Filling

200g mixed wild mushrooms, washed and chopped
2 banana shallots diced small
1 tbsp chopped tarragon
1 crushed garlic clove

Celeriac Coleslaw

2 large carrots peeled and cut to julienne
2 white onions sliced to julienne
½ celeriac sliced to julienne
(julienne - to cut into long, thin strips)
200ml crème fraiche
1 tbsp coarse grain mustard

Garnish

A few herbs for garnish
reduced balsamic for finishing

Method

For the pigeon

Heat a heavy bottomed pan, season the birds well then add some oil to the pan. When the pan is smoking hot seal the birds all over, add a knob of butter to the pan then baste the birds with the now foaming butter, transfer to a pre-heated oven at 160°C for 6 minutes.

It is very important to let the birds rest for at least 5 minutes before carving.

For the ravioli pasta

Mix everything together in a food processor, take out and knead to a smooth dough. Wrap in cling film and allow to rest for 30 minutes before use.

For the ravioli filling

Sauté the following together in some butter, mixed wild mushrooms, shallots, tarragon, crushed garlic clove, cool this mixture before making the ravioli.

Roll out the pasta very thin, do this twice so you have a bottom and top sheet, place little balls of mushroom mix onto one of the sheets then cover with the top sheet, mould the mounds of mushroom mix into raviolis and the cut them out with a pastry cutter.

Blanch the raviolis in boiling salted water for 1 minute and cool in iced water.

For the celeriac coleslaw

Mix the mustard with the crème fraiche. Blanch the celeriac, carrot and onion together in boiling salted water for 20 seconds and drain well, keep warm. Mix with the crème fraiche mixture just before serving.

To serve

Carve the breasts off the carcase and then slice each breast into thin slices, mix the coleslaw and put in the middle of the warm plate and arrange the pigeon around this, top with a ravioli and garnish with a few herbs and a drizzle of reduced balsamic. We also use a variety of winter vegetables to finish the dish.

DARK CHOCOLATE DELICE, EXTRA VIRGIN OLIVE OIL, HAZELNUTS, MILK ICE CREAM

SERVES 4

Method

For the chocolate delice

Melt the chocolate and the butter together. In a mixing bowl put the egg yolks and cocoa powder then whisk well and add the water. Slowly add the oil to make a chocolate mayonnaise. Soak the gelatine in cold water until soft and add to the melted chocolate. Mix the mayonnaise with the chocolate, then whisk in the egg whites, pour into desired mould. Chill until set. Portion into required size (this is very rich so a little goes a long way).

For the milk ice cream

Warm all ingredients in a saucepan (there is no need to boil) just to dissolve the sugars, allow to cool and churn in an ice cream machine.

To serve

In the restaurant we use the powdered hazelnuts as a base to serve the ice cream on, this stops the ice cream from sliding around. Assemble as seen in picture.

Ingredients

Chocolate Delice

300g 70% chocolate
25g butter
½ gelatine leaf
25g hot water
2 eggs yolks
5g cocoa powder
200g extra virgin olive oil
5 egg whites

Milk Ice Cream

600g whole milk
120g sugar
75g dextrose
100g pro-crema sosa
400g double cream

Garnish

50g powered hazelnuts
4 chocolate caramel tuille

158 SHIBDEN MILL INN

Shibden Mill Fold, Shibden, Halifax, West Yorkshire HX3 7UL

01422 365 840
www.shibdenmillinn.com

Shibden Mill nestles in the fold of West Yorkshire's Shibden Valley, an idyllic setting for this 17th Century 4 Star Inn, where it is surrounded by rolling countryside.

Owners, Simon and Caitlin Heaton have sensitively restored the historic property, which now presents 11 individually styled, stunning guest rooms; a cosy bar and dining area with low beamed ceilings and open fires, an upstairs restaurant and private dining.

The inn's reputation for fabulous food and warm hospitality extends far beyond the Yorkshire borders. Heading up things in the kitchen is Darren Parkinson (pictured right), a dynamic young man with an eye for excellence and innovative food combinations. The culinary team attracts wide spread acclaim for shaping dishes rich with inspiration, quality and diversity.

Working with the seasons forms the basis of a menu that presents the very best of whatever is being harvested at the time, with ingredients sourced locally to showcase the region's finest fish, poultry, game, meat, vegetables and fruit.

A wonderful selection of Cask Marque approved ales, including the Shibden Mill's own brew and an extensive wine list complement proceedings.

This splendid inn never fails to impress and is firmly positioned on the region's culinary map. The whole experience of dining and staying here makes planning your next visit a topic of conversation before you have even left.

The Inn's reputation for warm hospitality, premier gastro dining and first class accommodation draws people to the Shibden Valley from far and wide. For those stopping over in one of Shibden Mill's eleven luxurious guest rooms, there is much to explore nearby, however the beautiful surrounds of this elegant 17th Century property make it very easy to just relax and unwind. For those simply wishing to 'down tools' and indulge, once you have arrived and unpacked, there's no reason to leave

GRILLED MACKEREL, HANDPICKED WHITBY CRAB, CRISPY SMOKED EEL BOULANGÉRE POTATOES AND CAPER BERRY VELOUTÉ

SERVES 4

Method

Firstly wash and cut each fillet into two halves, season the crab meat with lemon zest, 2 teaspoons of juice, salt and pepper.

For the boulangére potatoes,

Slice each potato and layer into a small casserole pot or small sauce pan, lining it with wax paper and butter.

Add the smoked eel and sliced onion half way and continue to layer the potatoes with salt and pepper. Top with the rest of the butter and bake on gas mark 4 for 2 hours.

For the caper berry velouté sauce

Reduce the white wine, when reduced by half add the chicken stock and reduce by half again, then add the cream. Take off the heat and whisk in the mustard, capers and chives and set aside.

To serve

Grill the fillets of mackerel for 2 minutes. Cut the boulangére potatoes into four portions and place in the centre of your chosen plate. Next add the grilled mackerel and finally the crab. Garnish by spooning the caper berry cream around the plate to finish.

Ingredients

2 Mackerel fillets
200g white crab meat
1 lemon
5g chopped chives
5g butter
100g smoked eel
2 bakers potatoes
100g thinly sliced onion
100ml white wine
100ml chicken stock
100ml double cream
5g Lilliput capers
5g Dijon mustard
salt and pepper

ROAST "LEVEN FARM" DUCK BREAST, FIG TARTE TATIN, CONFIT CHERRIES AND PEAR PURÉE

SERVES 4

Ingredients

Roast Duck

2 free range duck breasts
thyme and garlic

Tart Tartin

2 figs
pre rolled puff pastry
10g butter
10g caster sugar

Confit Cherries

200g caster sugar
12 fresh cherries
half pint water

Pear Purée

1 large pear
100g sugar
50ml water
tbsp lemon juice

Method

For the confit cherries

Firstly make a stock syrup with 200 grams of sugar and the half pint of water by bringing to the boil and simmering for 5 minutes. Take off the heat and place all the cherries in the syrup and set aside for later.

For the tarte tatins

Place 10 grams of butter and 10 grams of sugar in a small tart mould, caramelise for a couple of minutes until golden brown in colour, adding the halved figs (cut from the centre down the middle of the fig so you have two halves of fig the same size) add the fig face down in the caramelised sugar in the centre of the mould, place the pre rolled puff pastry over the cooled fig and bring the edges over so they over lap and sit inside the tart mould. Bake for 15 minutes on gas mark 5.

For the duck

Pan fry the duck breasts skin side down in hot oil with the thyme and garlic for a couple of minutes, turn the heat down to low and continue to cook the breasts on their skin until nice and crispy, turn over and place in the oven on gas mark 5 for 8 minutes, bring out of the oven and rest.

For the pear purée

Peel, core and chop the pear into equal size cubes and add to a saucepan. Add the water, sugar and simmer until the pieces are soft. Mix in the lemon juice at the last minute and then blend in a liquidiser for a couple of minutes, set aside to cool down.

To serve

As seen in picture.

NORWOOD GREEN STRAWBERRIES AND ROSE WATER PARFAIT, SWEET WHITE BALSAMIC SYRUP AND SHORTBREAD BISCUITS

SERVES 4

Ingredients

Parfait

100g caster sugar
100ml water
4 egg yolks
5ml rose water
150ml double cream

Syrup

10ml white balsamic
125ml water
100g caster sugar
sprig of thyme

Shortbreads

450g salted butter
200g sugar
5g vanilla paste
500g strong plain flour

Strawberry Purée

200g strawberries
2 tsp lemon juice
100g caster sugar

Method

Start by making the shortbread

Firstly mix the butter and sugar together in a large bowl and beat with a wooden spoon until pale and smooth. Then mix the paste and flour, mix together for couple of minutes then place in the fridge to set and rest. After the shortbread has sat in the fridge for 10 minutes, roll out on a floured surface, until about 4mm thick and cut out 8 discs with pastry ring (120mmx45mm) and bake on gas mark 5 for 15 minutes. After cooking cool on a cooling wire.

For the parfait

Make a stock syrup with the sugar and water by bringing to the boil and simmering for one minute, then take off the heat and add the rose water. In a large bowl sat over a pan of simmering water whisk the egg yolks and sugar together, very slowly add the warm rose water syrup so you get a pale light creamy sabayon. Take off the heat and cool to room temperature, whisk up the cream and fold into the sabayon slowly with a large spoon.

For the stawberry purée

Make the purée by mixing the ingredients with a hand blender, add to the parfait mix and set aside.

In your pastry rings place the pre baked shortbread biscuit in the bottom and spoon the strawberry parfait mix on top. Top it off with another shortbread so it's like a sandwich in the ring. Make 4 rings up and place in the freezer for 3 hours to set.

For the sweet white balsamic syrup

Bring all the ingredients together and cool.

To serve

Take out of the rings, placing the parfait in the middle of the plate. Drizzle the white balsamic around the plate and garnish with icing sugar, halved strawberries and some purée.

168 WENTBRIDGE HOUSE HOTEL

The Great North Road, Wentbridge, Pontefract, West Yorkshire WF8 3JJ

01977 620 444
www.wentbridgehouse.co.uk

Wentbridge House is a beautiful Georgian country house hotel dating from 1700 and set in 20 acres of gardens and grounds in the village of Wentbridge, West Yorkshire. Steeped in history and surrounded by century-old trees, Wentbridge is a hidden gem and offers a luxurious and peaceful retreat from everyday life.

The hotel is independently owned and run with a great deal of care and dedication, ensuring the warm welcome, excellent service and restful atmosphere you would expect of a country house hotel.

Wentbridge House has always been passionate about food. Executive chef, Stephen Turner, and his team focus on delivering excellent food in a relaxed atmosphere which appeals both to hotel guests and the local community. The Fleur de Lys Restaurant is a true fine dining experience and holds 2 AA Rosettes. Local, seasonal produce and the best of British ingredients combine to create innovative and delicious dishes alongside one of the best and most extensive wine lists in Yorkshire, which features old favourites and a few surprises. The hugely popular Wentbridge Brasserie is slightly more contemporary and offers an alternative for those wanting simple, tasty comfort food in elegant surroundings.

Wentbridge House has been open since 1960 and continues to build an enviable reputation for excellence and was recently a finalist in the small hotel of the year, 'Welcome to Yorkshire White Rose Awards 2010'.

Images on pages p170, p172, p176 by Kev Rayner

Innovative, creative and passionate chefs preside over the Fleur de Lys Restaurant which attracts cosmopolitan lovers of food and wine. Emphasis is placed on using fresh, locally sourced produce and the best of British ingredients to produce a wide range of both classic and contemporary

SMOKED YORK HAM HOCK TERRINE, FOIE GRAS WITH ORCHARD APPLE CHUTNEY

SERVES 4

Ingredients

Ham Hock Terrine

3 smoked ham hock
2 sprigs of parsley
2 star anise
4 cloves
2 sprigs of thyme
1 bulb garlic
2 large carrots
2 celery sticks
1 white onion
2 leaves of gelatine
vegetable stock
8 slices of Parma ham
1 tsp Dijon mustard

Foie Gras

1 a grade foie gras (approximately 1¼ lb)
750ml good white wine
150ml water

Spiced Apple Chutney

225g chopped onions
900g apples cored and chopped
100g sultanas
15g paprika
15g mixed spice
15g salt
340g granulated sugar
425ml malt vinegar

Method

For the ham hock

Roughly chop the vegetables, garlic and herbs then colour slightly in a deep pan. Add ham hocks and cover with vegetable stock, simmer for 2 hours until ham falls off the bone. Remove all bone, fat and gristle. Add Dijon mustard, 50ml vegetable stock, 2 leaves of melted gelatine and then season to taste.

Place sliced Parma ham on a baking sheet and add the picked ham hock. Roll tightly to form a cylinder and cling film well.

For the foie gras

Leave foie gras at room temperature for 45 minutes so it is easier to work with. Remove all veins and bruised blood, season with salt and pepper. Shape the foie gras in a cylinder shape with a cheese cloth, and then tie at both ends.

Place foie gras in a small pan with wine and water, heat over a low heat until temperature reaches 180°F. Turn the foie gras over every 4 minutes, remove from the heat and leave to cool. (It is important to cook the foie gras slowly to reduce the loss of fat).

For the spiced apple chutney

Put all the ingredients into a preserving pan, slowly bring to the boil until the sugar has dissolved.

Simmer for 1½ - 2 hours, stirring occasionally. When it is very thick and you can draw a spoon across the base of the pan to leave a channel then you know that the chutney is ready.

To serve

As seen in picture.

POACHED HALIBUT WITH BUTTERNUT SQUASH PURÉE, KING PRAWN, VANILLA AND CHILLI BUTTER

SERVES 4

Method

Poach halibut in fish stock for 7 minutes until just firm to the touch.

Roast butternut squash, cut in half, score the flesh and roast until soft.

Remove flesh and then purée in a blender until very smooth.

Add a little fish stock if too thick.

Remove the seeds from the chilli and thinly slice the chilli.

Remove seeds from the vanilla pod.

Add to a little fish stock with the chilli and vanilla.

Add king prawns and reduce until the prawns are cooked.

Add butter to make a thick sauce.

To serve

As seen in picture

Ingredients

880g halibut loin
12 large black tiger prawns
2 butternut squash
100g butter
250ml fish stock
1 vanilla pod
½ red chilli
½ green chilli

WARM BERRY COMPOTE WITH FRAISE DE BOIS AND LEMON THYME ICE CREAM 'CANNELONI'

SERVES 4

Ingredients

Lemon Thyme Ice Cream

600ml milk
1 fat vanilla pod
6 egg yolks
150g caster sugar
100g lemon thyme

Tuille Paste

100g butter - melted
100g icing sugar
3 egg whites
100g flour

Simple Syrup

2 cups of water
2 cups of caster sugar

Berry Compote

12 raspberries
12 blackberries
12 small strawberries
12 fraise de bois (wild strawberries)

Method

For the lemon thyme ice cream

Pour milk into saucepan with the lemon thyme. Slice vanilla pod and remove seeds, then add to milk. Bring mixture almost to the boil, remove from heat and leave for 30 minutes to infuse the vanilla and lemon verbena. Beat 6 egg yolks and sugar until light and fluffy. Strain out the lemon thyme and vanilla pod then add mixture to milk, stirring until mixture forms a thin custard. Pour into a clean pan, set to a low heat while continuously stirring until custard mixture coats the back of a wooden spoon. Leave to cool for a further 30 minutes then add to ice cream machine.

For the tuille paste

Mix sieved icing sugar, flour and egg whites. Add butter and mix into smooth paste. Place a teaspoon of the tuille mixture onto a baking sheet lined with non-stick baking parchment. Bake for about 4 minutes on 190°C and then carefully wrap around a rolling pin whilst warm, to form a cylinder shape.

For the simple syrup

Bring the water and sugar to boil and reduce until syrup becomes sticky and thickens. Remove from the heat and leave to cool.

For the berry compote

Arrange berries in a deep bowl. Warm the syrup and pour around the berries.

To serve

Soften the ice cream so it can be piped into a cylinder shaped tuille, dust with icing sugar and place on top of the berries and serve.

RELISH YORKSHIRE LARDER

BAKERY

SIDE OVEN BAKERY
Carr House Farm, Foston-on-the-Wolds, Driffield
YO25 8BS 01262 488 376
www.sideoven.com

A range of homemade organic breads, croissants, honey toasted mueslis, juices and cordials. All wheat, spelt and oats are grown and processed on the farm using a stone ground mill. We aim to produce tasty foods with traditional flavours.

BEVERAGES

AMPLEFORTH ABBEY ORCHARD
Ambleforth YO62 4EN
01439 766 825
www.ampleforth.org.uk

Ampleforth Amber, cider brandy and sloe gin made by the Ampleforth monks and produced from the UK's most Northerly commercial orchard. Situated in the magnificent Howardian hills, the orchard has supplied apples to the local population for over 100 years.

HARVEY NICHOLS BORDEAUX SAUVIGNON BLANC 2009 – PLEASE NOTE THE VINTAGE WILL CHANGE
107-111 Briggate, Leeds LS1 6AZ
0113 204 8888
www.harveynichols.com

Pale lemon in appearance, this wine displays aromas of grapefruit, lime, elderflower and cut grass set against a backdrop of subtle mineral notes. On the palate, this crisp, mouth watering everyday white has a bright, fruit forward character that recalls flavours of citrus fruit and herbs.

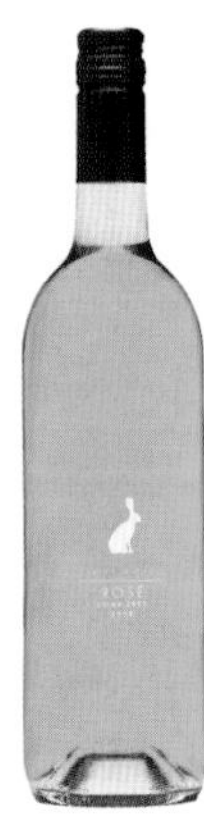

HARVEY NICHOLS ROSÉ 2009 – PLEASE NOTE THE VINTAGE WILL CHANGE

www.harveynichols.com

Produced via the Vin Gris method, our own label rosé, made from the indigenous red varieties of Grenache and Cinsault, is skilfully produced for us by Ollieux Romanis, one of the region's most revered estates. Salmon-pink in colour, the nose is graced with subtle, engaging notes of dried flora, red fruit and mixed herbs, leading to understated flavours of raspberry ripple, strawberry shortcake and an assortment of regional spices. Delicious on its own, this versatile rosé is also the perfect accompaniment to lightly flavoured shellfish, poultry and pasta dishes.

COOKING SCHOOLS

SWINTON PARK COOKERY SCHOOL
Swinton Park, Masham, Ripon, HG4 4JH
01765 680 900
www.swintonpark.com

Housed in Swinton Park's beautiful converted Georgian stables, and using ingredients from the estate and walled garden, the Cookery School course programme offers a choice of day and residential courses run by award-winning Cookery School chef Robert Taylor and celebrity chef Rosemary Shrager.

DAIRY

MICHAEL LEE FINE CHEESES
Unit 9 Lister Park, Green Lane Ind Estate, Featherstone, West Yorkshire WF7 6FE
01977 798012
www.finecheesesltd.co.uk

Known as the cheese champion to many of his clients, Yorkshire born Michael Lee is an expert at offering advice on gourmet cheese selection and cheese board recommendations.

SHEPHERDS PURSE CHEESES
Leachfield Grange, Newsham, Thirsk YO7 4DJ
01845 587 220
www.shepherdspurse.co.uk

Award-winning cheeses made from cows, ewes and water buffalo milk including the delicious Bells Bluemin White.

YEE KWAN LTD
Unit 2 Devonshire Business Park, Sheffield S1 4HX
07971 492 671
www.yeekwan.com

This family run business producing luxury handcrafted ice cream and sorbets, specialising in oriental flavours. A lot of love and care goes into creating delicious Far Eastern-inspired recipes, deliciouslyorkshire dairy product winner for its Black Sesame Seed Ice Cream.

YUMMY YORKSHIRE ICE CREAM
Delph House Farm, Denby Dales, Huddersfield HD8 8XY
01226 762 551
www.yorkshiremilk.co.uk

Suppliers of ice cream and dairy products.

FARM SHOPS

BALLOON TREE FARMSHOP AND CAFE
Stamford Bridge Road, Gate, Helmsley, York YO41 1NB
01759 373 023
www.theballoontree.co.uk

Deliciouslyorkshire best retailer of regional produce winner. Renowned farmshop and cafe supplying super fresh fruit and vegetables – specialising in seasonal asparagus and strawberries when available. Award-winning bakery and in-house kitchen supply meals to the cafe.

BEADLAM GRANGE FARMSHOP AND TEAROOM
Beadlam Grange, Pockley, York YO62 7TD
01439 770 303
www.beadlamgrange.co.uk

Deliciouslyorkshire best use of regional produce tearoom award winner. Also award-winning farmshop. Customers can enjoy a unique farm shopping experience in lovely traditional surroundings. Excellent butchers counters with home produced meal and deli counter selling vegetables, chutneys and cheeses. Try the delicious home-cooked food in the Granary Tearoom.

FINE & SPECIALITY FOODS

CASA MIA ONLINE

Unit 9 Buslingthorpe Green Trading Estate, Off Meanwood Road, Leeds, West Yorkshire LS7 2HG
0845 688 1818
www.casamiaonline.com

Casa Mia Online sell only the best authentic Italian brands and products from wines, champagne, spirits, coffee, teas, cheeses, preserved vegetables, chocolates and much more. We also make our very own fresh Italian style bread.

HARVEY NICHOLS EXTRA VIRGIN OIL

107-111 Briggate, Leeds LS1 6AZ
0113 204 8888
www.harveynichols.com

Harvey Nichols Extra Virgin Olive Oil is produced on the Colonna estate in Molise, Central Italy. A selection of the finest olives, predominantly Frantoio, Peranzana and Leccino are blended to give a herby, grassy flavoured oil with an elegant peppery aftertaste, creating a perfect balance between strength and elegance.

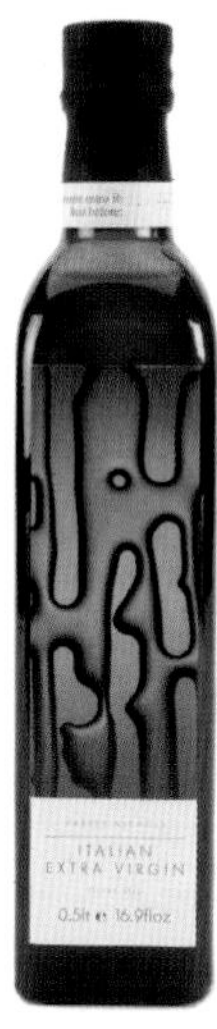

HARVEY NICHOLS RHUBARB AND ORANGE PRESERVE 340G

Harvey Nichols Preserves are made in small handmade batches to traditional recipes that are close to 100 years old. Harvey Nichols Yorkshire Rhubarb and Orange Preserve contains pieces of rhubarb in this citrus spread, that combines the sweet earthy taste of rhubarb with a sharp tang. The rhubarb is grown in the Rhubarb Triangle in West Yorkshire.

HARVEY NICHOLS SUN DRIED TOMATO PESTO 270G

Ligurian basil and sun-dried tomatoes are mixed with nuts, olive oil and garlic to make Harvey Nichols Red Pesto. Delicious on canapés, or mixed with cream or crème fraiche as a pasta sauce.

HARVEY NICHOLS TAGLIATELLE PASTA 500G

Harvey Nichols Tagliatelle pasta is a thin noodle like pasta. Our sources tell us that tagliatelle was created by a talented court chef in 1487 who was inspired by Annibale II Bentivoglio's hairdo so should be the fashionista's pasta of choice! Our tagliatelle comes in coils and is made by traditional methods using the finest ingredients, then passed through bronze moulds to form the shapes and dried very slowly.

FISH

JCS FISH

Murray Street, Fish Docks, Grimsby DN31 3RD
07764 157 046
www.jcsfish.co.uk

Salmon specialists who aim to supply delicious, high quality, fresh and frozen salmon at competitive prices. Deliciouslyorkshire award winner for its skinless boned mint marinated salmon portions.

SAILBRAND

Unit 11-15, Block C, New Wholesale Market, Red Doles Lane, Huddersfield HD2 1YF
0845 227 0066
www.sailbrand.co.uk

Provide a varied and exotic range of produce from native fish, meats and game to exotic seafood, continental sausages and cheeses.

SCARBOROUGH SHELL AND FISH COMPANY

Market Hall, St Helen's Square, Scarborough YO11 1EU
01723 372 782
www.shellandfish.co.uk

A seafood equivalent to a farm shop. Providing sustainable caught fish (long line) and shellfish caught by our own and other local boats. Also ethically killed shellfish.

MEAT

ANNAS HAPPY TROTTERS

Burland, Holme Road, Howden East Yorkshire DN14 7LY
01430 433 030
www.annashappytrotters.com

Our pigs enjoy a free range livestyle from beginning to end.Being part of only 2% of pigs reared in this way in the UK they are undoubtedly lucky, well looked after pigs. The quality of meat from our pigs is second to none.

DORIC GAME LTD
151 Buslingthorpe Lane, Leeds LS7 2DF
0113 2392 400
www.doricgame.co.uk

Suppliers of meat poultry and game. Our team of qualified catering butchers are fully experienced in preparing a full range of meats to the highest standards .

GEO MIDDLEMISS AND SONS
3 Market Street, Otley LS21 3AF
01943 462 611
www.dalesnet.co.uk

Another deliciouslyorkshire award winner for its Yorkshire Pastrami. Traditional award-winning butchers shop established in 1881. Located in the heart of the thriving market town of Otley and specialising in locally sourced beef, lamb and pork.

HARTLEY BUTCHERS
Richmond House, Tholthorpe, York YO61 1SN
01347 838 337

ROUND GREEN FARM
Worsbrough, Barnsley S75 3DR
01226 205577
www.roundgreenfarm.co.uk

Suppliers of home reared venison and venison products to individual and commercial clients.

PRESERVES

ROSEBUD PRESERVES
Rosebud Farm, Healy Masham, Ripon HG4 4LH
01765 689 174
www.rosebudpreserves.co.uk

Producer of sweet and savoury preserves since 1989. Our preserves are made by hand, in small batches, using traditional methods and are characterised by bold, fresh flavours and natural sets.

SMOKED FOODS

BLEIKERS SMOKEHOUSE
Unit 88, Glasshouses Mill, Glasshouses, Harrogate HG3 5QH 01423 711 411
www.bleikerssmokehouse.co.uk

Traditionally cure and smoke a broad range of the finest quality fresh fish. At Bleiker's we're passionate about creating innovative and above all tasty smoked fish whilst remaining faithful to the authentic recipes and know-how, brought to Britain by our founder Jürg Bleiker. Our provenance and quality is recognised by numerous awards from the Guild of Fine Food Retailers.

SWEET FOODS

LA DOLCE ITALIA
Unit 9 Buslingthorpe Green Trading Estate, Off Meanwood Road, Leeds, West Yorkshire LS7 2HG
0113 262 3322
www.ladolceitalia.co.uk

La Dolce Italia is not just about the very highest quality of product, the best in reliability and service... but the knowledge that all La Dolce Italia stands for, is the best and only the best. We supply an array of traditional and Italian cakes and desserts from Gateauxs to Homemade Cheesecake, Roulade, Continental decorated desserts and Neapolitan Patisseries.

SCIOLTI BOTANICAL CHOCOLATES
PO Box 88, Brigg DN20 8WT
07927 028 734
www.scioltichocolates.com

Handcrafted chocolates made by Fiona Sciolti using natural botanical flavours, real fruits, teas, herbs, local cream and honey. Deliciouslyorkshire winner for its Real Mint Thins.

CONTRIBUTORS

1885 THE RESTAURANT

The Recreation Ground, Stainland, Halifax HX4 9HF
01422 373 030
www.1885therestaurant.co.uk

ALDWARK ARMS

Aldwark, North Yorkshire YO61 1UB
01347 838 324
www.aldwarkarms.co.uk

ANTHONY'S THE RESTAURANT

19 Boar Lane, Leeds LS1 6EA
0113 2455 922
www.anthonysrestaurant.co.uk

THE BLUE BICYCLE

34 Fossgate, York YO1 9TA
01904 673 990
www.thebluebicycle.com

THE BURLINGTON

The Devonshire Arms, Bolton Abbey, Near Skipton BD23 6AJ
01756 710 441
www.thedevonshirearms.co.uk

THE BUTCHERS ARMS

38 Towngate, Hepworth, Holmfirth, Huddersfield HD9 1TE
01484 682 361
www.thebutchersarmshepworth.co.uk

CASA MIA MILLENNIUM

Millennium Square, Leeds LS2 3AD
0113 245 4121
www.casamiaonline.co.uk

EL GATO NEGRO TAPAS

Oldham Road, Ripponden, Sowerby Bridge HX6 4DN
01422 823 070
www.elgatonegrotapas.co.uk

ESTBEK HOUSE

East Row, Sandsend, Whitby, North Yorkshire YO21 3SU
01947 893 424
www.estbekhouse.co.uk

THE FOURTH FLOOR CAFÉ AND BAR

107-111 Briggate, Leeds LS1 6AZ
0113 204 8000
www.harveynichols.com

THE HEPWORTH

Sheffield Road, Near Hepworth, Holmfirth HD9 7TP
01484 683 775
www.thehepworth.co.uk

HOTEL DU VIN & BISTRO

88 The Mount, York YO24 1AX
01904 557 350
www.hotelduvin.com

THE OLD VICARAGE

Ridgeway Moor, Ridgeway Village, Near Sheffield S12 3XW
01142 475 814
www.theoldvicarage.co.uk

THE PIPE AND GLASS INN

West End, South Dalton, Beverley, East Yorkshire HU17 7PN
01430 810 246
www.pipeandglass.co.uk

SAMUEL'S AT SWINTON PARK

Swinton Park, Masham, Ripon, North Yorkshire HG4 4JH
01765 680 900
www.swintonpark.com

SHIBDEN MILL INN

Shibden Mill Fold, Shibden, Halifax, West Yorkshire HX3 7UL
01422 365 840
www.shibdenmillinn.com

WENTBRIDGE HOUSE HOTEL

The Great North Road, Wentbridge, Pontefract WF8 3JJ
01977 620 444
www.wentbridgehouse.co.uk

MORE QUALITY RECIPE BOOKS AVAILABLE FROM THIS PUBLISHER

Relish Yorkshire Second Helping – Featuring a foreword by Celebrity Chef Tessa Bramley. This second edition features yet more recipes from Yorkshire's finest chefs including Michelin Starred James Mackenzie from The Pipe and Glass Inn, Michelin Starred Steve Smith from The Devonshire Arms, Anthony Flinn of Anthony's Restaurant and Richard Allen from The Fourth Floor at Harvey Nichols to name a few. A must have for any food lover with a connection with Yorkshire.

Relish Cumbria – Over 50 exclusive recipes from some of Cumbria's finest country house hotels and award-winning restaurants including Nigel Mendham at The Samling, Russell Plowman at Gilpin Lodge Hotel and Andrew McGeorge at Rampsbeck Country House Hotel plus many more. Packed with innovative recipe ideas and stunning photography, Relish Cumbria makes a fantastic addition to your cookbook library.

Relish Scotland – Over 300 Pages of Scotland's finest chefs recipes. With breathtaking pictures of the views and venues at these highly acclaimed Scottish restaurants. This book takes you on a journey from Edinburgh to Glasgow, across to Aberdeen and up to the Highlands and Islands. Featuring an introduction from TV celebrity chef Nick Nairn and recipes from Scotland's finest chefs including no fewer than six that are Michelin Starred. Relish Scotland promises to make very interesting reading to foodies and tourists alike.

To find out more about these publications and about the restaurants featured please visit www.relishpublications.co.uk